MAKE A FORTUNE

SELLING

TO

WOMEN

THE DEAL MAKERS *and* DEAL BREAKERS YOU
MUST KNOW TO CLOSE THE DEAL EVERY TIME!

CONNIE PODESTA

GREENLEAF
BOOK GROUP PRESS

Published by Greenleaf Book Group Press
Austin, TX
www.greenleafbookgroup.com

Distributed by Greenleaf Book Group LLC

For ordering information or special discounts for bulk purchases, please contact Greenleaf Book Group LLC at PO Box 91869, Austin, TX 78709, (512) 891-6100.

Design and composition by Greenleaf Book Group LLC
Cover design by Greenleaf Book Group LLC

Publisher's Cataloging-In-Publication Data
(Prepared by The Donohue Group, Inc.)

Podesta, Connie.
    Make a fortune selling to women : the deal makers and deal breakers you must know to close the deal every time / Connie Podesta. – 1st ed.

    p. ; cm.

    ISBN-13: 978-1-929774-90-6
    ISBN-10: 1-929774-90-7

1. Women consumers--United States. 2. Consumer behavior--United States. 3. Women--United States--Attitudes. 4. Marketing--United States. I. Title.

HC79.C6 P63 2009

658.8/34/082   2008941986

Part of the Tree Neutral™ program, which offsets the number
of trees consumed in the production and printing of this book
by taking proactive steps, such as planting trees in direct proportion
to the number of trees used: www.treeneutral.com

TreeNeutral

Printed in the United States of America on acid-free paper

09 10 11 12 13 14   10 9 8 7 6 5 4 3 2 1

First Edition

Contents

Introduction

What do I know about you? I know your biggest worry is *not* closing the deal, *not* making the sale, *losing* the customer. I know that what you want more than anything is to be able to determine what the customer wants or needs in order to make the decision to buy from you. I also know your biggest frustration is trying to understand *why* a customer took her business elsewhere or decided not to buy at all. These are pretty universal fears, doubts, and worries that come with the territory of sales.

As a salesperson, you are probably very interested in learning about anything and everything you might be doing (or not doing), saying (or not saying), and even thinking (or not thinking) that might cause one of your female customers or potential customers to *not* buy from you. These things are the demons of the sales industry. They are

DEAL BREAKERS

Pretty scary things, these deal breakers, because they usually remain hidden, invisible to us even when we're actually using them in the sales process. Even worse, they are painfully apparent to buyers. It's a salesperson's biggest nightmare: we are doing exactly the opposite of what the customer wants—and we don't even know it! And, unfortunately, the customer probably won't tell us what we are doing wrong. So how do we ever change our behavior and attitudes and become better salespeople when honest feedback is so hard to come by? That's what this book is all about. I promise to tell you exactly what you need to know about what women really want and expect when it comes to buying from you.

Think back to the past and picture a female customer walking (hopefully not running) away from you and a potential sale. You thought you had it made, the deal was in your pocket, the contract was all but signed, when suddenly it was over—she was gone and she wouldn't return your calls. And what she said as she walked out doesn't help you at all, clichéd phrases like "I decided to go another direction" or "It's just not the right time for me now" or "I think I'll look around a little more." Worse yet is that you have the feeling that she will probably make the purchase from your competitor next week. Those are the moments when we just don't get it. "What happened?" you say to yourself. "Everything seemed to be going along just fine." Well, it wasn't—you just didn't know it. To help you identify these undiscovered deal breakers, I'm going to take you inside the mind of a woman who wants to buy—and you are going to discover exactly what to do to make sure she buys from *you*.

First, we must remember that making a sale is a very fragile process—much more fragile than most salespeople think or would like to believe. I find it interesting that the majority of sales books and training programs either don't recognize this fact or they simply ignore it, bombarding salespeople with aggressive techniques to get the customer, keep the customer, and close the deal. But from a psychological standpoint, the success of any sale hinges much more on what you do wrong than on what you do right. It's a lot like trust. A person can do many things to earn your trust, but it only takes one thoughtless act to undo the trust that was built. Sales is just as unforgiving. Consequently, it is imperative that you recognize and understand what it is that you might be doing or saying that may drive her away—what deal breakers you may be committing unknowingly—so you can change and move on to greater levels of success. As soon as you understand what *doesn't* work with women and *why* it doesn't work, you'll be ready to make your female customers your best, most loyal customers of all.

So what kills sales with women? Well, what many skilled, intelligent salespeople don't realize is that some of the most elusive deal breakers may be originating from the gender lens they and their customers are looking through. If you're using techniques that work for men when you're selling to women, you're going to lose a lot of sales—sales that could easily have been yours. And guess what? Using female-oriented techniques on male customers isn't going to work, either.

Right now, you may be coming back with a very politically correct thought, like "I treat men and women exactly the same." Well, if that's actually true, and I doubt that it is, then that's exactly why you're losing sales—to both genders. What is more likely is that you do sell to men and women differently, but you've never identified how or, more important, why. There is no plan in your mind for how to approach each differently, so you just resort to the techniques that work *most* of the time.

I am about to become your new best friend—at least in the area of successfully selling to women. And I think you will find that I can help you a lot with your male customers as well. I am committed enough to your success to tell you the truth about what it is you might be doing that turns your female customers away and what you need to do to not only make the sale but also keep customers returning time after time. Let there be no doubt about it: female customers are absolutely vital to your business—no matter what your industry. And the sooner you know what the deal breakers are when selling to women, the sooner you can stop losing sales unnecessarily and begin to enjoy and profit from your business.

"Classic" Techniques Are Killing Your Success

Let's cut to the chase. Women, for the most part, shop differently and buy differently than men. Unfortunately, sales training hasn't changed much in the past fifty years. The training you got when you started in sales was probably designed by men for male salespeople selling to male customers or to female customers without full decision-making ability. But the sales landscape has changed dramatically and continues to do so.

You probably have more and more female customers every day, and that is only going to increase as time goes by.

Not only do women now control their finances directly, they are also purchasing services that were historically purchased by men. You'll see more and more women at garages, golf shops, and hardware stores, as well as making major buying decisions in industries such as agriculture, technology, finance, and insurance. So if you think that it's unlikely that in your specific industry you will need to worry about how to sell your product to women, you're wrong. And losing out on their business will cost you in terms of money, sales, and reputation, both now and in the long term.

Plus, most women are great customers to have. I realize that the perception is often the opposite—especially for the salespeople just trying to make a quick sale. Sometimes a salesman will say to me, "Connie, you know I love women, right? But come on. They take up a lot of precious time. They worry about each and every little detail. And they talk too much: They tell us their life stories trying to explain what it is they're looking for. We don't need that. Just tell us what you want and we'll give it to you." So some salespeople have preconceived ideas about which behaviors are an acceptable part of the sales process and which ones aren't.

Give me a quarter and I'll guess the typical sales approach: contact the customer, do a needs assessment, overcome all objections, close the deal. Seems like a perfectly respectable process, right? Well, it's certainly a formula that has been around a *long* time. However, there's one big problem. This approach doesn't work with most women, or with a lot of today's men either! It is definitely time for a change in both strategy and delivery.

Sales just isn't that cut-and-dried anymore. Customers expect much more from their sales experiences, regardless of gender. They have done their homework, have a better understanding of what they want and need, and they have many choices in terms of what to buy and whom to buy from. Ultimately, they want the sales experience to be suited to their needs and desires. If it isn't, they can quickly and easily find an establishment or salesperson who will make it happen. So you can't just pull a sales approach out of some outdated sales training manual—especially when it comes to women. Instead, you have to be intuitive, creative, spontaneous, responsive, and flexible.

 You have to understand that your sales technique has to be different every time with each and every person.

This book is about exploring all of the wonderful advantages and potential a female customer can bring to the relationship so you do not miss out on tons of customers with lots of money to spend with you.

What Do Women Customers Bring to the Table?

Women influence the majority of all buying decisions. En masse, they are an absolute powerhouse market for you. They have money, and they are willing and able to spend it—hopefully, with you.

They *do* love to talk—to you, but more important, *about* you. Once you have established a great relationship with a female customer, she will tell everyone she knows about you and your product. She is the best advertisement money could buy. How often do you hear men talk to each other about their best buying experiences? Rarely, if ever. You can rest assured that when you sell to a woman, she will "sell" *you* in return.

If women like you and trust you, they *will* return and will probably bring friends and relatives. (How many men have come back with their buddies to introduce you?) Women, as you may have heard, *love* long-term commitments, and sales isn't any different. Since men are more results driven, they often go where they see the best price tag and may or may not even remember your name after the deal has closed.

Women not only buy for themselves, they also buy for other people. They are always thinking about what their kids want, their friends would like, and their coworkers need. When they see a deal or meet a salesperson they like, they'll likely spread the word, even if they don't buy that product or need that salesperson. They want to share their good fortune with everyone.

Women are usually very appreciative and satisfied when they are able to make a purchase that is right for them and fits their needs. And, as a result, they are willing to share that with you, the salesperson. So it's rather fun to close a deal with a woman because she lets you know that she got what she wanted, and she is glad you helped her through the process.

So not only are women vital to your sales, they also have a lot of added bonuses that make them very good customers—customers well worth the time it takes to understand better. And this is where understanding basic gender differences is critical.

Women and Men Are Different

It certainly isn't a news flash that women and men are different. But the important thing here is that not only are women and men different in how they communicate, they are also very different in how they approach shopping and buying. I've been a therapist, a professional speaker, an executive coach, and a saleswoman for more than twenty years, and much of my work has centered on the fact that, for the most part, men and women don't think alike, talk alike, communicate alike, express feelings alike, negotiate the same, or even show emotion in the same way. And those differences in style, perception, attitudes, and expectations carry straight into the selling arena.

So what are the basic differences between men and women when it comes to buying styles?

1. Men are most often "results" buyers. They are focused on the transaction and the end results. Although they are engaged in the process of the sale, they are more forgiving (or may not even notice) if the experience isn't everything they expected as long as they believe they are getting exactly what they

wanted. When they do focus on the process, it is in terms of the results—how they can get what they want for less, or with more, or faster.

2. Women are mainly "experience" buyers. They look at the process of a sale in its entirety and are engaged in each step along the way. They can be easily dissuaded from continuing the process at any point if they see signs that something is wrong (especially if these signs come from the salesperson). Each stage of the process is being judged and evaluated. They maintain a long-term focus, and the results are important primarily in context of the entire experience.

Am I saying that all women buy alike and all men buy alike? Not at all. So before you send an e-mail explaining that it's either unfair or impossible to stereotype men and women and that each person is a unique individual, I'll save you some time and tell you up front that I agree completely. After working with people as long as I have, I readily admit that, indeed, each and every person is different. I'm not saying that women don't care about results (they do!), just that they are usually less results focused than men. I'm not saying men don't care about the experience (they do!), just that they are often less experience focused than women.

That said, *many* women and *many* men share the generalities I outlined above. But remember, I've already said that to be successful in sales, you have to be intuitive, creative, spontaneous, responsive, and flexible. In fact, the best salespeople have highly intuitive natures and are extremely imaginative when it comes to switching strategies when necessary. With a little practice looking at your female customers through this lens, you'll be able to tell what will work and what won't. And with a little practice looking and listening for the cues I'm going to identify for you, you'll recognize them when they show up in your male customers, too.

If You're a Saleswoman, You Should Still Read This Book

Let me be clear on one thing right up front: This book isn't just written for men. There are plenty of women selling to other women who may not be using the right approach to close the deal. Remember what I said: most sales training is still based on techniques that are male-centric and often outdated. So, unfortunately, many saleswomen can be just as guilty as the men when it comes to selling to the results buyer rather than the experience buyer. So every salesman and saleswoman needs to be able to identify and reassess any and all strategies they are currently using that could possibly turn off or turn away their female customers.

 Just because you are a woman doesn't mean that you intuitively understand how to sell to women.

In some ways, this book is more important for you than for your male colleagues. I'm sure you already have figured this out, but it won't hurt to remind you—women will always be harder on you, less forgiving of you, and take it more personally when you let them down or misread them than when men do. Women naturally expect other women to understand their needs better than men do—so you're on the spot, and you have to make sure you really can understand their needs. Not to mention the fact that your female customers are sizing you up faster than your male customers.

This might also be a good time to mention that, throughout the book, I devote a fair amount of time to the buying and shopping habits of men—just to help clarify the differences between men and women. So to both my male and female readers: you will definitely learn a few things about selling to men that you may never have heard before as well. Ah . . . two books for the price of one.

How I Can Help

I'm going to lay it out for you. I'm going to tell you what women usually want compared to what men usually want, what you're doing that may negatively influence or have an impact on her desire to buy from you (deal breakers), and then we will focus on exactly how you can change your sales style and techniques to turn those deal breakers into deal makers. And be warned: anytime we prepare to move to a different level of expertise and understanding, you'll be expected to do a bit of self-evaluation. That is probably the toughest part for those of us in sales. Healthy egos give us the confidence necessary to be successful in sales; however, our egos also make it more difficult for us to assess ourselves critically and be open to new ways of thinking, acting, and behaving. I can imagine that there will be times throughout this book when you might be inclined to read what I've written and say, "I would never do that" or "I don't think that way" or "No one would ever see me like that." But if you have ever lost a sale to a woman, odds are you said or did something that she considered to be a deal breaker. Now the key is to understand why, when, and how that might happen.

So in preparation for some upcoming self-analysis, let me ask you some important questions. Do you want to build a better female clientele? Do you want to close more deals with women? Do you want more repeat business from your female customers? If so, then it's time to be honest with yourself. To help you be more objective about what you might need to change or do differently,

I am going to start each chapter with questions for you to think about. Be as honest as you can about how you would react, feel, or think when you answer each one. And then use the chapter to discover ways you can put what you need to know into action—to help you and your female customers have productive and long-lasting relationships.

What else do I know about you? I know that you are very busy and your time is valuable. Like you, I understand the importance of quick access to immediately useable information that will help attract new customers, keep existing customers, better negotiate sales, and close more deals. That's what I am going to give you. I'm counting on the fact that you are confident enough to try some new things and take a new approach. That doesn't mean you have to eliminate all the great techniques you've already developed— just have an open mind. Realize that, unfortunately, some of the strategies that you are most proud of may be exactly the things that drive some women away.

So adopt the golden rule (at least of this book):

 There is no right or wrong way to buy, but there is a right and wrong way to sell to each kind of buyer.

Because that, ladies and gentlemen, is exactly what you are about to learn.

What Women Want

FIVE WAYS TO CLOSE MORE SALES WITH WOMEN

QUIZ

Be honest!

1. Based on your experiences, make a quick list in your head of five words that you think describe the sales process a woman is looking for.

2. What percentage of sales would you guess are influenced by women?

3. A woman walks into your office or store wearing sweatpants and a torn T-shirt and has three kids in tow. What's your gut response?

4. True or false: With a woman, you've got a better chance of convincing her to buy if you emphasize the "soft" benefits of your product rather than the "hard" details of how your product compares to the competition.

5. What is it about your products or services that make them attractive to women? Is your product so strong that women will buy it regardless of who is selling it?

6. Women like to talk during the sales process. So when you're selling to a woman, what types of things do you talk about to get her to feel comfortable? The weather? Your kids? Other customers? Personal information from your life? Or just the product?

7. Think about the last time you weren't able to close a sale with a female customer. What were the exact reasons the sale fell through?

When you've finished reading this chapter, think about these questions again and see whether your answers are different.

If you're a man, I bet you're thinking that this chapter alone could be worth the price of the book—and you might just be right. Figuring out what women (and men) want has been an interesting project of mine for decades (and will probably continue to keep me busy for years to come). The good news is that there are definitely specific keys to understanding both men and women that will help you be more successful during the sales process. If you're a woman, you probably know what women want in a personal relationship, but you may not have a clue as to what they want as buyers. Even though you have been a buyer yourself, it's doubtful you stepped back during a shopping experience and analyzed how and why you did what you did. It's also hard to separate your personal experiences into general rules without talking to lots of other women about what they look for when they're buying. But if you take all that information and boil it down to the bottom line, you come up with one of the most important differences between selling to men and selling to women:

With a man, you can concentrate on *closing* the sale.

With a woman, you had better concentrate on *committing* yourself to the sale.

With her, it is critical that you commit to the entire sales process, rather than focusing on just the end result. In other words, the typical aggressive sales techniques that have been the core and mainstay of sales training for decades will probably *turn her off*, which will then *turn her away from you!*

So, are you ready to enter the fascinating, complex, and as much as I hate to admit it, sometimes confusing mind of a woman shopper? Then let's start with some great news.

I recognize how busy you are, so I'll begin this chapter by saving you one full hour of unnecessary time and reading.

Most books on selling to women spend at least the first chapter or two (1) convincing you of how important women are as customers because of their enormous buying power; (2) giving you case study after case study of companies that learned the hard way that they had to advertise, market, and sell differently to women; and (3) offering lots of statistics, charts, and graphs supporting right- and left-brain theories of communication, the history of gender differences, and the growth of women's purchasing power. And after an hour, you have yet to learn one single thing that you can use tomorrow to help you make more money and be more successful. Since I trust that you are smart and already know that women are critical to the success of your business or career, I thought you might like me to sum up all of that information in a few sentences so we can get right down to the business of helping you close and commit to more deals (and make more money—no apology for that being a major goal as well).

We can begin by eliminating at least twenty pages of statistics, numbers, data, and research. There is only one statistic you really need to know (and believe):

 85 percent of all consumer buying decisions are made or influenced by women.

No other statistic can compare to this one. No other statistic is necessary in order for you to dramatically increase your "sales to women" percentage. Women are either buying for themselves, buying for someone else, or telling someone else what to buy 85 percent of the time something gets sold! Wow! Now you can begin to understand why this book is so vitally important to your future success in sales.

Now allow me to save you thirty more pages of charts, graphs, and useless case studies by giving you the bottom line when selling to women: It is a documented reality that, psychologically, women tend to think, act, communicate, negotiate, listen, socialize, make decisions, and *shop* differently than men. Therefore, it's a fact of life that those of us in sales need to adjust our styles of selling to accommodate those differences if we ever want to be successful selling to women.

Why is this important? Because it means there is *big* money, *amazing* potential, and *outstanding* long-term sales relationships in your future if you understand how to sell to women in a way that recognizes and speaks to their unique approach to buying.

Now let's get to work.

Remember, women are usually the experience buyers. They are mentally critiquing each stage of the process and constantly evaluating whether to stay in or get out. After interviewing and talking with hundreds of women of all ages, backgrounds, cultures, and socioeconomic groups, I quickly realized that women have a very specific set of criteria and expectations in mind when it comes to how they want their buying experience to *feel*. (And, by the way, you might as well get used to hearing the word *feel*, because you'll see it a lot in this book.) Emotions, feelings, and a sense of personal connection are some of the biggest differences between male and female buying styles—women develop feelings about every aspect of the process and those feelings drive their decision to buy from you—or not buy from you. So you have to be able to apply that knowledge when selling to women. If you are a "feelings" kind of person already, you are several steps ahead in the game. If you aren't, then selling to women will be more of a challenge, but don't worry—I'll teach you exactly what you will need to do to have that more "personal" touch without leaving your comfort zone.

If there is one question that men have asked more than any other—more than "How can I earn a million dollars?" or "How can I live longer?" or "How can I achieve wealth, fame, and success?" it is simply "*What* do women want?"

But that's a question for another book, and maybe you saleswomen out there aren't as interested. So for this book, let's amend the question to ask: What do women want to experience as a buyer in order to commit to the sale?

Throughout my research, women have told me good stories and bad about their shopping experiences. They told me what they wanted and what they didn't want, what they needed and didn't need, what they liked and didn't like, and what they expected and didn't get. Almost everything they described fell into one of the following five categories.

What Women Want:

- They want the experience to be PERSONAL
- They want the experience to be PROFESSIONAL
- They want the experience to be PRODUCTIVE
- They want to be PART OF THE PROCESS
- They want the experience to be POSITIVE

These are the five key elements needed to create the most desirable buying experience for a woman. Let's look at each one up close to get a better idea of what women want from their shopping experiences.

She Wants the Experience to Be Personal

The first thing you need to know (and accept) when selling to a woman is the following:

 It's not just business, it's personal.

Anyone who says that business isn't personal doesn't know women at all. For most women the decision to buy is based on many personal beliefs, perceptions, ideas, memories, and most of all—you guessed it—feelings.

Let's face it, no matter who you're selling to, sales requires personal encounters with discussions about what someone PERSONALLY wants or needs, and success is reinforced and sustained by continuing a long-term PERSONAL relationship with each customer whenever possible. It begins the moment those first personal questions are asked: What do you want? What do you need? How can I help you? How can I make you richer, happier, healthier, or more successful?

We salespeople ask both men (results buyers) and women (experience buyers) these same questions. The difference is that women are more aware of the PERSONAL side to sales and will make very quick decisions during this initial interview process about whether a salesperson seems sincere, acts courteously, and treats them appropriately, and whether they will feel comfortable doing business with that salesperson. They size the situation up in terms of *how* they want to buy, whereas men tend to focus on *what* they want to buy. The same holds true for communication. Women focus on *how* something is said and men focus on *what* is being said.

Women also tend to be very personally connected to their purchases. I honestly believe that a great many of the purchases women make are directly related to something that is worrying them, and the purchase is made to bring relief—the car is getting old and not safe so let's take it in, the roof might leak so let's fix it first, the kids need clothes, office supplies are low, this old computer might crash, or I want to make sure we can travel when we retire so let's invest. A good example is when my husband and I were exploring different options for a new will. He was not at all excited about the whole process: he can't drive it, eat it, play with it, or sleep on it. Plus, he said it was depressing to think about and not a fun way to spend money. Left to himself, I think making a will would have remained on his "to do when nothing else in the world is going on" list forever. Basically he was there to buy a service—not because he wanted it, but because I did. This is a perfect example of how women influence men to buy. I, on the other hand, felt we were *personally* (see, there's that word we women like to use) responsible for making sure that everyone was taken care of in the event of our deaths. I didn't think it was fun either, but I was eager to get it done so I could stop worrying about it.

When we met with our estate planner, I brought a huge load of emotion into the meeting—my family, my feelings of responsibility, memories, concerns about doing the right thing by everybody, fears about how I would live without my husband, thoughts about what would happen if I died first (would he remarry, how long would it take him to remarry . . . I got a bit off track). I was also remembering what happened when the relative of a friend died without an up-to-date will: it caused much confusion, heartache, and jealousy among the remaining family members. I wanted to find a person to help me prepare my will who would understand *all* of those factors. My head was swimming as we walked in.

Are men and women different? You bet! I guarantee you *none* of those thoughts were going through my husband's mind! In fact, when I asked him what he was thinking he said, "I should have parked under a tree where it's shady if we're going to be in here very long so the car won't get hot."

As I walked into the office, I was concerned about much more than the bottom line—in fact, details and cost were not even in my thoughts at that point. I wanted to make certain that this particular estate planner was willing to listen and then integrate everything I wanted and needed, not just simply write up a will. I wanted him to have a thorough understanding of all my needs, concerns, worries, and goals so he could create the perfect scenario for us. I was PERSONALLY involved from the beginning of the meeting, even though we hadn't even decided whether or not to use his services. From the moment I was introduced I was aware of each nuance of the process. I immediately began to look for clues as to how I would be treated and whether this was someone I wanted to continue to do business with. Let there be no doubt—I was conducting an interview based on how he reacted to my PERSONAL needs and expectations.

My husband, on the other hand, was sitting quietly, waiting to see what was going to happen, and reserving judgment on the details until he had a chance to hear the facts and get a handle on the bottom line. He was focused on the end results and I was focused on the entire experience. I began "judging" the salesperson way before my husband did.

Like me, many women are looking to accomplish much more in their relationship with a salesperson than finding someone to take their orders. Therefore, you *must* be aware from the very first second how much weight a woman is placing on *who* she does business with. A woman wants to do business with someone she likes and trusts, someone she feels comfortable with, and someone who she believes she can count on. (Important note: Making the shopping experience PERSONAL for a woman does not mean being flirtatious, overly intimate, or in any way sexual—ever. That's a deal breaker that goes without saying.) While a man might put up with an unfriendly auto mechanic known for excellent work and great prices, a woman won't. She'll pay a little more and take her car to someone she likes and who treats her with respect—as long as she's still confident he or she can get the job done. If she's not satisfied with the second mechanic, she'll go to a third and a fourth until she finds someone she can be confident and comfortable doing business with. When you're doing business with women, you have to be better than the next guy!

A woman's need for a personal experience means that feelings, the connection between salesperson and buyer, and the possibility for a long-term relationship take precedence in the sales process and are much more important than you might expect.

I know a couple who moved into our neighborhood a few years ago from an area about thirty minutes away. She still drives the half hour to her hairdresser, dry cleaner, drugstore, and gym. We have all of these services within a block of our house, but it's worth the drive to her to continue to use people she feels "connected" to, people she has developed personal relationships with.

Her husband, on the other hand, took no time at all discovering the closest places and switched his services immediately. He discovered he could get the results he needed right around the corner. But since she's focused on the experience instead of just the results, a female buyer is much more likely to stay loyal, even if it means being slightly inconvenienced.

Quick tip: If you want to sell to women, learning to invest in and manage the PERSONAL aspects of the process is critical to your success.

She Wants the Experience to Be Professional

Even though women usually want their sales experience to be PERSONAL, that does not mean they don't also expect it to be PROFESSIONAL. In fact, in order for her to accept and be comfortable with a PERSONAL shopping experience, it must also pass the test of being PROFESSIONAL. Most women are savvy shoppers and will ultimately be focused on making a good, intelligent, and price-conscious decision, regardless of their personal feelings—it's just that you will have to pass the PERSONAL test before she can move to the next step. Ideally, the two will go hand-in-hand, but don't think you can play on her emotions to get her to make a purchase that isn't in her best interests.

It has often been said that with women, emotion drives reason, and with men, reason drives emotion. I don't think this is giving women nearly enough credit. Women couldn't be where they are today if they constantly allowed emotion to take precedence over common sense and value. But it's worth noting how much women can do and process at the same time. They can be evaluating the personal side of the experience: Do they feel respected? Do they like you? Do you like them? Are you friendly? Are you enjoyable to be around? And at the very same time, they can be weighing other critical factors: your experience and credentials, the value of the product, the quality of the service, and whether you can be trusted. So when I tell you that a woman wants the experience to be personal, don't underestimate her absolute need for a professional experience. Both weigh heavily in her decision to continue the sales relationship with you.

Ultimately, every woman is looking for a professional-grade deal. Think of professionalism as one aspect of your brand. That attribute means that everything will be open and aboveboard (no shady financing deals or merchandise that fell off a truck). It means you'll stand behind your product, she won't have to haggle and hassle to get the same deal her friend got last week, and if and when something goes wrong, you'll accept responsibility and take care of it efficiently and professionally.

Professionalism, for many women, is shorthand for safety—physical, emotional, and financial safety. If women don't feel safe with you, your establishment, or with the deal they're making, they will stop listening and start watching—everything and everyone. They will switch from looking for a good deal to looking for a good exit strategy. Your professionalism is a reflection of your personality, attitudes, and respect for yourself and others. So the first issue is your female customers' level of comfort with you. This is all about your level of respect, trust, and commitment. How you look at her, where you look at her (always aim for the eyes), the tone of your voice, and the manner in which you conduct business are all clues her radar will pick up quickly to determine whether this will be a comfortable and professional situation in which to do business.

I have not talked to a single woman who didn't have at least one story of a salesperson who made her so nervous or uncomfortable that she couldn't get away fast enough.

I have had several encounters with unprofessional behavior, but one comes to mind. Years ago, when my husband and I were buying a house after moving to a new city, I did most of the looking on my own while he worked. The first realtor I dealt with was a woman who had me running away from her by the end of the morning. She certainly knew her territory and had an uncanny gift of figuring out exactly what we were looking for, but she wasn't professional at all and made me very uncomfortable. She constantly talked about her other clients and the money they had (or didn't have) to spend. Then at every house we viewed, she would tell me very personal things about the neighbors. Even though she knew her product and had an excellent grasp of what we needed, I felt she shared too much confidential information. I knew if we bought from her, it was just a matter of time before her gossip would include us and our personal information.

> You must respect her time, her space, her privacy, her personal information, and her intelligence.

Being professional also means you're qualified, knowledgeable, and experienced—you're representing your product/service and company competently and she doesn't need to check you out from every angle to make sure you won't try to cheat her or take advantage of her. You know where the lines are and you stay within them. Boundaries are important to a woman and you need to recognize and respect hers.

This professionalism is pretty critical stuff, because if she isn't comfortable with you, the environment, or the deal, she's going to take her business elsewhere, and you will probably never know why.

She Wants the Experience
to Be Productive

Men are busy, but women are really, really busy! Why are women busier than men? In all my years of educating, interviewing, and counseling, it always boils down to one major difference between us and the guys: women have an always-on generator for worry and guilt, and those two emotions generate a mental to-do list that never ends. Women are like a computer with a hundred tasks minimized at the bottom of the screen ready to be "pulled up" and dealt with at any given moment. When my husband walks from the bedroom to the kitchen to get a drink of water, it's a simple task. He goes, gets what he needs, and returns. Sounds easy, doesn't it? When I go on the same errand I return thirty minutes later after doing eight other things on my way to the kitchen. My mind sees into nooks and crannies, closets and cabinets, inside and out. And I usually come back without what I went after because the task took on a life of its own. Men often say (and they have a point) that we women create our own "busyness" and we should just stop worrying. A woman's answer is always, "If I stop worrying, nothing will get done around here."

This worry and guilt springs from a belief that many women hold: it is their job or responsibility to make sure everyone else is happy, healthy, and successful—or, at least, that they could make it happen by working just a little harder. I often tell my audiences that men live in the present—what is going on now? how do I feel now? what can we do about it now?—whereas women live mostly in the past and the future. The past is guilt: what we shoulda, woulda, coulda done differently. The future is worry: what might happen, could happen, probably will happen. Most men are far better at compartmentalizing and tuning in or out depending on what they view as necessary or important that requires their immediate attention. Women view the world more holistically. It's more than just multitasking—it's multi-seeing, multi-hearing, multi-doing, and multi-fixing all at once. Almost everything we see and hear reminds us of ten other things, which remind us of ten other things each. So the word *busy* doesn't begin to describe life through a woman's eyes—whether the busyness is self-imposed or not.

What does all of this have to do with sales? Everything! Because she has so many things she needs to do or thinks she needs to do, your female customer doesn't have time to waste (unless she is window shopping, which is an entirely different experience in itself—but she won't involve you in that).

Many salespeople make the mistake of focusing more on productivity with their male shoppers than with their female shoppers. The truth is that women don't want to waste their time any more than men.

It is true that when men are looking to buy, they go in, find what they want at the price they want to pay, and get on with their lives. Therefore, salespeople know right from the beginning that men have little patience with the buying process and would rather be somewhere else—anywhere else. As a result, the astute salesperson gets right to the point with the guys and moves quickly to the bottom line, unless there is an indication that the man prefers to take a bit more time.

Women, on the other hand, usually take far longer to make a purchase. They ask more questions and spend more time weighing their options than men. Salespeople often misinterpret this to mean that a woman is "just shopping around," has all the time in the world, or is simply indecisive. As a result, the salesperson will often tune out the woman who appears to be just looking and perhaps even wander off and move on to someone else. Be very careful making any of those assumptions, because you could be way off base. She probably is taking longer because she sees the purchase as part of a bigger picture and she wants to make sure it is going to fit in with whatever else is going on in her life. The sound system she's buying needs to offer great performance, portability for her daughter's college move next year, and adaptability for new technology two years from now, and it has to match the living room decor. Thinking through all those things at once just takes a little time!

Even though a female customer may take longer to close or commit, she still doesn't want to waste any of the time she has allotted for the purchase—she has just allotted more time to begin with than a man would. But that doesn't mean she wants to be ignored, get passed from salesperson to salesperson, or repeat herself to a salesperson who wasn't paying attention the first time. Never underestimate how precious a commodity time is for a woman. Anything you can do to help her find the right solution to fit her needs will be appreciated. Anything you do to derail the process will be noted and chalked up against you. This is true even though she may appear more social than productive and decisive at first while she is trying to assess whether she likes you, trusts you, and wants to do business with you. This is part of her PER-SONAL and PROFESSIONAL examination of you and the situation at hand. Once she has decided that you are the right person to do the job, she will probably do an about-face and get down to business. Let her take the lead. She'll let you know when she is ready to start buying. You just concentrate on being personable, professional, and productive.

She Wants to Be Part of the Process

For most women, a purchase isn't just a transaction in which she pays money for the goods or services on offer. It's an entry into a relationship—with you, with your store, with your product or service, and with your company. Because business is PERSONAL with women, if they choose your service, it's often because they are comfortable supporting your business, representing your brand, or becoming part of the circle of your customers. Women are aware that their purchasing decisions reflect back on them and affect the world they live in; this is just part of the multifaceted approach women take to buying.

Maybe it's because of this awareness that women feel the need to take responsibility for their buying decisions—they don't want to just walk in and buy something ("In and out," a man might say). They want to weigh the options, learn the differences between them, and decide what's best. They want the information that will help them make good decisions. Women hate to waste time making purchases they will regret, not use, or have to return later. They want to know what makes one brand or product better than another—or why you think one will be better, and whether it really is or not.

 In short, women want to be a part of the process and have good interaction with the salesperson.

Now don't get me wrong—men want to be part of the process too, but most salespeople wouldn't dream of excluding a man from a conversation about his purchase. Again there is irony here. Men talk less in the average buying situation, ask fewer questions, and are more anxious to just leave and get on with it than women, yet men are generally included in each step of the process whether they want to be or not. Women, who tell their whole story, ask tons of questions, and have often done far more research on the product, can find themselves excluded from some conversations because the salesperson has decided that the information is too difficult, tedious, technical, or uninteresting to share with her. Beware of making one too many assumptions about what a woman wants to know and learn about your product or service, because if she feels left out of the process, you will lose the sale more often than not.

Being part of the process means more than just being engaged in all decisions and understanding the variables. It also means being listened to—a point we are going to discuss a great deal throughout this book. It means that when a woman wants to explain why she wants something or how it needs to fit into her life, you listen, even if you think you already have the information you need. (If she's still talking, there's a good chance you can still learn something to your advantage about what she wants and why. Pay attention!)

 When she asks a question, answer it honestly, without getting irritated or impatient, and give her an answer that's as complete as she needs.

A great example of being excluded from the process is something that most of you can relate to—and it happens to men and women equally, although for some reason it doesn't seem to bother men as much as it bothers women. I absolutely *hate* it when I am buying a car and the salesperson gets up in the middle of our negotiation and goes back to the "manager's" office. Because the offices are glass, I can see them huddled over papers making very important notations and scribbling frantically. Then the salesperson comes back and gives me the "absolute best deal his manager has authorized him to give." No way! That's when I say, "I want to deal with the manager or whoever else has the authority to talk, discuss, negotiate a fair price that works for me, get me the paperwork, and hand me the keys." I want the person who can do it all *without* leaving me out of the process.

I asked my husband about this once (he was the one doing the buying that time, so I didn't feel it was my place to interfere . . . much). I asked him why he put up with them doing this. He simply said, "Cuz that's the way they do it." "But it's stupid and silly," I said. "Oh, it doesn't bother me. I'll get the price I want and the car I want anyway. It's just part of the game." "But it's wasting our time!" I replied. You know what he said?! "We didn't have much to do today anyway."

Now we buy cars separately. I like my way and he likes his. I go in, get the person who can make the deal, tell him or her what car I want and the price I'm willing to pay (after doing lots of research), drive the car, and pick the color. I sign the papers and I drive out. If the salesperson isn't comfortable with involving me to that level, I find someone who is!

Making your customer part of the process means that the end result is a good deal for both sides, not just your side. It means that you're her ally, not her competitor. This desire to be part of the process is a key reason why high-pressure sales approaches typically don't work with women. If she feels pressured, if she feels that you're pushing a deal that's going to benefit you a lot more than it will benefit her, then she will quickly peg you as someone who is not her ally, not her advocate, and not someone she will trust to help her make the very best decision for her.

The best way to tell if you're making her part of the process is to ask yourself if you are involved in a sales pitch or a sales dialogue. If she isn't talking, asking questions, and following closely along with what you say, she's probably waiting for you to stop talking so she can say no or make an excuse to simply leave and go elsewhere.

Remember, when a woman becomes silent in a sales transaction—it's probably *not* good news for you!

She Wants the Experience to Be Positive

Fact: A woman shops for one of the following two reasons: because she *has* to (groceries, school supplies, cleaning products, car repairs, insurance policies) or because she *wants* to (furniture, plants, clothes, art, shoes, presents). In both cases, however, the experience had better be POSITIVE. When she doesn't want to be shopping because she has a thousand other things to do or it's not something she really cares about, she will be sensitive to anything that makes the situation worse: hard-to-find parking, annoying music, lack of attention, products out of stock. And when she is shopping for fun, she will resent anything that makes the situation less than pleasant.

What's the difference between that and what men experience? Men seldom *want* to shop or view it as fun (with the exception of a few things that support their hobbies: cars, motorcycles, sporting goods, electronics, etc.). A man usually expects the process to be boring, mundane, confrontational, and a royal pain in the neck. So he's not disappointed when it is. He is also not as tuned in to the environment as she is. He notices long lines, high prices, and what time it is, but he's pretty well tunnel-visioned about getting through the line and out the door. While she's in line (or waiting in your office) she is aware of the colors, the music, the furniture, the displays, the other customers—anything and everything that adds or takes away from the total experience.

But while a man might judge a shopping experience solely on convenience, for a woman, the most important component is the sales interaction. The essential criteria for determining whether the experience is positive or not rests on you—your attitude, your personality, your style, your smile, your enthusiasm, your commitment to service, and the way you handle the sale itself. It is up to you to set the tone and establish an atmosphere that is conducive to making good purchasing decisions. Her favorite shopping ambience is one that is relaxed, cooperative, and hassle-free.

Women are not big fans of playing the game when it comes to negotiating the deal. We don't find it part of a POSITIVE and pleasant experience. That's not to say a woman won't do or say what's necessary to get the right and fair price, but when she *has* to shop, she wants to pay the price and get going. And when she *wants* to shop, she doesn't want to be embroiled in an argument over price or a product or defend what she wants or needs to buy—that will only destroy the mood and excitement of the moment.

The really good news is that one of the best side effects of a positive buying experience is that it is the fastest way to earn referrals from your female customers. If they get what they want out of a purchase, but feel ambivalent about the experience, they may or may not recommend you or your establishment to their friends. But if they get what they want and they had a positive experience, you're sure to get referrals. Why? Because women love to talk—they will criticize you to anyone and everyone when the experience is negative, but they'll rave about you to everyone when it's great!

Women, far more than men, will be your biggest advertisers, supporters, and promoters if given something great to talk about.

So exactly what factors determine whether a sales environment is positive? First, take a brutally honest look around you: your company and its vision and reputation, your customer service policy, the quality of your product or service, your product's relevance to your customers, your guarantees, and your culture. Next, take an equally close look at yourself: your attitude, your commitment to service, your listening skills, your confidence level, your social skills, your health, your sense of humor—and the list goes on. There are a lot of things that must be present for an environment—and an experience—to be considered positive. And I do know that as a salesperson, you can't afford to be mediocre or middle-of-the-road. You have to create a memorable, POSITIVE impression.

A great example of the differences in sales experiences—positive versus negative—happened right before my husband and I were taking a cruise to Alaska. We had never been to Alaska before, but some friends had made the trip and had given us a list of excursions we just "had" to take: everything from zip-lining and hiking to bear watching and dog sledding. Just one problem. We live in Dallas—we had absolutely no appropriate clothing or equipment for any of these activities. So I headed to the biggest sports store in the area, a monolithic, three-story sports mecca. I didn't have a clue what to buy or even where to begin.

I approached a saleswoman who was talking on the phone and waited. Finally she looked up and I told her my situation. "Over there," she said, pointing behind me. "Excuse me?" I asked. "Go over there and you'll find all the hiking stuff." "But I need more than just hiking gear, and I don't know what hiking gear I need," I said. "Well," she said, "I'll be over before you finish and then I'll show you where to go next." Feeling confused, I walked to the hiking department and began picking up anything and everything that looked like it might work—gloves, long underwear, boots, even goggles. A young salesman spotted me, came over, and offered to take a few things out of my arms. He looked at what I was carrying and asked jokingly if I was preparing for a trip around the world. No, I laughed, but then I suddenly became a bit unglued.

I told him that I had signed up for all these cruise excursions and now I had no idea what I was doing. I wished I was just staying on the boat relaxing by the pool instead of hiking into the wilderness unprepared. Oh, and by the way, did they sell bear repellent?

The young man was silent for a moment, and then he did the perfect thing. He smiled, calmly led me to a chair, set all my items in a pile, and said, "Okay, we are just going to sit here for awhile and figure this out." I was beginning to feel that he was taking a PERSONAL interest in my trip. "Let me see your itinerary so I can take you mentally through this entire week. I have been to Alaska many times, and by the time we are done you will not only have everything you need, but you will feel totally comfortable doing all the things you have signed up to do." With these words, he was assuring me that the time spent with him would be very PRODUCTIVE and that I would definitely be a PART OF THE PROCESS.

Over the next hour, he not only explained and described each and every excursion I was taking, but he also had his associate go and get the clothes necessary for that particular event. He had an incredible amount of PROFESSIONAL knowledge about the products I would need, and he kept my list to the necessities. It was a very POSITIVE way to spend the afternoon, and it was the perfect sales experience for me. I have been raving about him to everyone I meet. I even gave his name to my travel company and cruise director. And yes, both the original saleswoman I spoke with and the young man were on commission. Though how the woman was making a living in sales is beyond me.

 When a sales experience meets *all five* criteria it is a slam dunk.

Are you totally excited yet? I hope so! This is an exciting business. I absolutely *love* sales. Well, let me amend that—I *love* sales when I make the sale, and I feel downright terrible when I don't. But that doesn't happen too often anymore. Why? Because I've pretty well figured out what works and what doesn't, what turns people on and what turns people off!

Successful sales is about making tough assessments about yourself and your relationships with other people and then being willing and able to change the things that don't work.

It's about taking ownership and not blaming the prices, the economy, the customer, or the corporate office.

Ready to close and commit to more deals with women? Ready to learn more about yourself? Excited to understand more about what makes women buy and shop the way they do so you can use that information to create and sustain long-term relationships with female buyers? Yes, there are a lot of elements to consider when selling to women, but they're all related, too. To help you understand how to apply these principles, we're going to jump into the deal breakers that will kill a sale with a woman, applying these principles as we discuss them. By telling you what not to do, we'll really be showing you ways in which you might be violating these principles and driving women away. So get ready to analyze your present sales strategies and perhaps substitute some exciting and profitable new ones!

Deal Breaker #1

SHE DOESN'T WANT TO PLAY THE GAME

QUIZ

Be honest!

1. You are helping a female customer choose between two products. One is 50 percent more expensive than the other, but the cheaper one is a better fit for her needs. If she buys from you and chooses the less expensive option, will you see it as a successful or unsuccessful sale? What if she chooses the more expensive option?

2. When you make a sale, do you feel like doing a victory dance or congratulating your customer?

3. Have you ever used the following sales techniques?
    *   Flooding your customer with information
    *   Intimidating or pressuring your customer with the consequences of not making a decision
    *   Acting irritated when your customer asks for too much information or takes too long to make a decision
    *   Telling your customer that the offer is only good until the end of the day when that's not true

4. You're getting nowhere with a female client. She seems locked in indecision and there are other clients you could be helping, other sales you could be closing. How do you get her to move forward? What techniques do you use to get her to close?

What do you think of when you think of games? Competition, right? The excitement of the struggle? Giving it your all? Or that mother of all thrills—VICTORY!

Guess what? Most women do not want any of this when it comes to the buying experience. None. They do not want to compete against you, wrangling for the best deal. They do not want the process to be difficult or a test of endurance. They do not want a clash of wills. They don't want it to take a lot of energy. And they certainly do not want to "lose" so that you can "win"—in fact, they don't even want *you* to lose so that they can win. Women spend their entire lives trying to keep themselves and the people they care about from having to experience disappointment, hurt, loss, and unhappiness. As a result, most women don't find anything fun at all about the prospect of having to compete to win at someone else's expense while trying to make a purchase—nor do they want to do business with someone who has that mindset.

Now don't get me wrong—women are certainly capable enough and willing enough to negotiate, haggle, and debate to get a good deal. We do it all the time and love to walk away with a great bargain. And there is no doubt that women can be extremely competitive in certain situations. But unlike men, we do not try to turn the sale into a sport. Listen to the language of men in sales situations: "I scored a big client," "I made a killing," "I beat him at his own game," or "He didn't know what hit him."

 The big difference is that men like to battle and conquer their opponents and women want to talk and figure out a solution.

The main difference between men and women in this case is that when a man is buying, not only is he willing to play the game, he also *expects* to play the game. He would be disappointed and have little respect for the salesperson not "up for the challenge." Even though he knows that the salesperson is trying to get the better of him, he feels confident that he will win out in the end: he'll get the better deal, he'll get you to lower the price more than you wanted to, he'll maneuver you into throwing in more extras. It doesn't matter how he's keeping score as long as he thinks he's ahead.

Although women can be masterful scorekeepers in relationships, they will seldom find scorekeeping appealing when making a purchase.

For most men, negotiating is about winning, getting the upper hand, and wearing someone down. For most women it's about talking, resolving, and discussing the options in a nonhostile way. Women are far likelier to judge situations as "healthy" (sane, functional, stress-free) versus "unhealthy" (combative, confrontational, manipulative). If a woman views the transaction as argumentative, she may withdraw altogether and find a situation where she can purchase in a healthier environment.

Think about using the five attributes of what a woman wants in a buying situation and you'll quickly understand why turning the sales process into a competition is a misfire at every level.

PERSONAL: It's hard to develop a personal connection with a competitor. We avoid getting close to our competition because we are trying to beat them rather than befriend them. We understand they will do almost anything to win.

PROFESSIONAL: Women want two-way communication that is honest and open. They don't want to worry about seeming weak or vulnerable. But if you are her competitor, then opening up to you would be the last thing a woman would do. And she can't expect the same from you, either.

PRODUCTIVE: She doesn't have the time or energy to play games. She wants this to be a collaboration, not a competition. Game playing simply takes precious time away from her busy schedule.

PART OF THE PROCESS: A female customer needs to feel that you are there to help her, not steer her into a solution that you think is best just because it's easier or more profitable for you. If this is a game to you, you're likely going to let her play only on your terms.

POSITIVE: Competing in a fight to the death is not fun at all! In fact, it's disconcerting and stressful as far as most women are concerned.

She doesn't want an intense game of pickup, she wants an ally. She wants you to be friendly, knowledgeable, and a good listener with her best interests at heart. That means stepping away from the playing field and putting on your thinking cap.

Tip #1: Don't Use Manipulation as a Tool to Make a Sale

For a woman, game playing and manipulation are really one and the same. Manipulation is your way of trying to control the playing field by changing her perceptions, and it necessitates a competitive approach to the sale. Think about it—would you manipulate someone you see as being on your team? No, because that would mean leading them to see something that isn't there, or ignoring something that is. It would be both foolish and self-destructive to manipulate someone who was on your own team because it would weaken your own potential for success. The key to being part of a successful team is knowing that if the team loses, you lose too. Somewhat counterintuitive to the traditional sales approach, right? Believe me, most women will quickly recognize an attempt to manipulate them and will know exactly what it means—that you're not interested in a PERSONAL connection except to exploit it, you don't want her to truly be PART OF THE PROCESS because you have your own agenda, and you're only interested in making the experience PRODUCTIVE for yourself.

Of course, in sales we try to please and enhance all of the senses to make our products (and ourselves) seem as good as we can make them. And that means controlling how our products are shown, how our customer is treated, and how the environment sets a mood. We definitely want to influence a customer's decision in our favor. The hottest cars are placed right in the middle of the showroom. The lights are set to make every product shine and gleam. Soft, upbeat music plays in the background while we shop. These are all subtle but expected forms of influence, and salespeople rely on these techniques to give them additional sales power. But we aren't fooled into thinking something is better than it is by the lights, or the shiny chrome, or the smell of fresh coffee, or the relaxing music. In fact, we find it rather enjoyable to be offered cool drinks and ushered into a well-decorated office while enjoying a view of the best products offered. This isn't stressful or confrontational or misleading. But women want no such "staging" effects in the PERSONAL relationship. For a woman, there is a big difference between subtlety and deceit, between staging an environment and being controlled and manipulated.

I remember interviewing a financial planner a few years ago who was the master of manipulation. I spent an hour with him and would have left much earlier, but I was fascinated by his use of every cheesy, manipulative technique in the book, so I basically stayed to watch the show. When I walked in, my favorite vanilla latte was waiting for me. He had called and asked my secretary what my favorite drink was. Okay, that was staging at its best, and I admired these little extra touches—at first! But then he started with the compliments—how young I looked to own my own business, how talented I must be to be in professional speaking. Give me a break. That was the set up. I knew what was coming next, and sure enough, once he thought he had me swooning and compliant, he moved into the real pitch. He adopted a fatherly voice, leaned over, and said, "But if you want to continue living the lifestyle you are living right now, there are some serious problems with your portfolio." Now that the scare tactics had been initiated, he quickly entered the rescuer phase and told me not to worry, because he could fix everything with just a few minor changes in mutual funds—at a cost I wouldn't even notice down the road.

I just sat quietly and waited to see what would come next. It was the "gang" technique. He pressed a button and two other men and a woman entered; he introduced them as the team that had assessed my situation and would help me get back on track. He then handed me a shiny, four-color report with pie charts and bar graphs and statistics. "Now don't let all these numbers confuse you," he said. "That's why we're here: to make this as easy on you as possible." If I wasn't offended already, he took it a step further and launched into the upsell—I needed a new will, new insurance, basically new everything. I already had these things, so he either hadn't listened when I told him or thought that he could make me believe I had made a series of bad choices.

Women don't need flattery, compliments, scare tactics, or patronizing reassurances. They don't want gimmicks and tricks. Attempts to manipulate a woman are taken PERSONALLY: she will feel insulted and disrespected. She will not view you as her ally, her collaborator, or the person who will help her solve her problems; she will view you as the opponent who is out to make the sale no matter what the cost to her. When she begins to see you as a hurdle, it will be easier for her to find somebody else to deal with rather than waste the time trying to go over or around you.

Of course, there are more passive ways of manipulating buyers as well. Sometimes I have been in situations where the salesperson goes on and on with so much information—most of which is irrelevant at this point in the process—that I have found myself almost ready to buy just to get out of there. Then I realize that, consciously or unconsciously, the salesperson is exhausting me as a way of manipulating the sale. Excessively complex processes, options, and features have the same effect. While these forms of manipulation don't necessarily inspire the same anger that the more confrontational versions do, they're still annoying and likely to turn off female customers. She wants to feel like PART OF THE PROCESS, and that means you should never be too long-winded or involved in the nitty-gritty until and unless she asks for that level of detail.

Keep it simple! That doesn't mean dumb down your information, just streamline your information and processes and make them as easy as possible. Even though women have the reputation of loving to shop, they certainly don't *love* a confrontational, confusing, or complicated shopping experience. And our golden statistic—women make or influence 85 percent of all purchases— also shows us that women are often buying things that aren't fun at all. They're buying service plans, financial services, insurance policies, groceries, office equipment, landscaping materials, and appliances. So don't try to wear her down and bury her under loads of information she doesn't need in order to manipulate the sale. If you overwhelm her with unnecessary facts and figures, she probably won't buy.

 Make yourself available to her if she wants additional information, but make sure the buying process is structured around her.

If you can make your environment nonmanipulative and hassle free, you'll encourage female buyers to stay longer, ask more questions, become more involved and committed to the product, and ultimately get more excited about making a purchase—all of which leads them to buying more, both now and in the future. It's harnessing the POSITIVE possibilities for your business instead of the negative. What buyer wouldn't prefer that? I can guarantee you that a woman will.

Tip #2: Keep the Pressure Off

As salespeople, we don't necessarily like to admit to pressuring our customers to close a deal, but we have probably all done it at some time or another—even when we didn't mean to. Customers know we do it. Many of our ploys are obvious, organized, and expected. "These prices won't last long, so come in today!" announcers shout in radio and television ads. And customers know that, most likely, those prices will last much longer than advertised. In fact, customers—particularly male customers—pressure salespeople right back to lower prices, offer better financing, or throw in extras. I have a male friend who lives in a hot climate. With any new car purchase, he negotiates a price and then, just before he signs the contract, he says, "Oh, and I'm not going to sign unless you throw in window tinting." And they always do.

In essence, many forms of pressure are perceived to be perfectly respectable forms of negotiation. But, as with manipulation, there's subtle pressure that is often expected, and there's devious or negative pressure that can make customers feel anxious, bad about their buying decisions, or unsure about their decision to work with you. And those are not PRODUCTIVE or POSITIVE feelings.

When selling to women, the first problem with applying pressure is that women react to pressure differently than men, so you need to carefully anticipate that reaction and adapt your sales approach accordingly. The second problem is that salespeople often use different pressure tactics with women. And when those efforts are heavy-handed or result in negative feelings, women are more likely to run than succumb.

From a woman's perspective, sales pressure just adds to her already harried, stressful day and brings on feelings of guilt and worry—neither of which puts her in the mood for buying.

She doesn't just have to manage all the elements of the purchase she's making, she also has to manage you, keeping you off her back as she tries to make the best decision for her. This requires more of her time and energy and in the end is less PRODUCTIVE. The easiest way for a woman to make the process more efficient is to find someone more amenable, patient, and helpful to guide her to the close.

So instead of using high-pressure sales techniques, try to give her time and information. The most PRODUCTIVE use of a woman's time in a sales situation is allowing her to make a smart decision, regardless of how long that takes. The problem is that for you, the most productive use of your time is to get to the close—as quickly as possible. But if you use artificial deadlines ("We're only offering this price today"), rush her to sign before she understands all aspects of the deal, or use any other tactics to get to the close before she wants to be there, you'll likely never get there. If there are real deadlines that she is facing, let her know about them up front, as soon as you know she's seriously considering the product—that will let her know you're thinking ahead and not just trying to pressure her.

Another kind of pressure, the very worst kind, is bully pressure. The theory is that because many women like to avoid conflict and soothe sore feelings, they'll do anything an irritated, intimidating salesperson wants, just to diffuse the situation. Some salespeople allow their annoyance or irritation to show during the sale, hoping to push a female customer into buying more quickly. These sales bullies act impatient with or insulted by questions, implying that the customer is taking too long and wasting their time. Sometimes, salespeople take on a superior manner, an I-know-better-than-you-little-lady attitude, to try and drive their female customer into the deals they want to close. Please be on notice that people who bully others into submission have very low self-esteem, although they would be the first to tell you otherwise.

Confident people *never* have to resort to bullying or aggressive tactics to get what they want or to make a sale.

Bullying is about power and intimidation—not about service or helping people get what they need. This type of pressure doesn't sit well with women at all. First, women don't buy well when stressed-out, and it is definitely not fun to make a purchase when someone seems irritated, annoyed, or impatient with you while you are trying to make a decision. Second, women aren't just put off by bullying tactics, they're usually downright insulted. Remember how important it is to make her PART OF THE PROCESS? This is the opposite—trying to shove her into doing it your way, with as much negative force as you can deliver. Plus, it's rude, disrespectful, and completely unprofessional to bully a customer—man or woman.

I recently noticed that my back tire was low so I decided to stop in at the dealership near my house. It took quite a while to get waited on, and then as I tried to explain to the service manager what the problem seemed to be, he cut me off and said, "You probably need a new tire. We can get to it in a couple of hours." He then walked away, leaving me standing there. Well, I needed more information before I made that decision, so I stepped over hoses and car parts to follow him, saying, "Could you just check it first to make sure it just doesn't need some air?" He rolled his eyes and said, "Lady, I've been doing this for twenty years. If you think you know more about cars than I do, then you're welcome to fix it yourself. But I can tell you by looking at it, you need a new tire—in fact, probably two new tires on the back." He managed to insult me and upsell me in one breath. So I took the car down the road where a very nice gentleman put some air in the tire, told me to forget about the fee, and sent me on my way. Bullies only drive women to find a more comfortable place to do business.

Instead of being argumentative, defensive, or combative (even unintentionally), be the calm in the storm, the voice of reason, the one who can make it happen smoothly and effortlessly. A peaceful, rational environment is hard to come by, and it will keep your female customers buying again and again.

Tip #3: Win Without Competing

Now you might be saying, "But, Connie, you are missing the biggest incentive component to the whole ideas of sales. Sales is based on winning and the competitive spirit!" I agree. Most sales are referred to as "wins." Individuals, teams, and departments are in constant competition with one another to see who can sell the most, who can improve the most, who can win that trip to Maui. In fact, competition is what gives structure to sales, and it adds that indescribable rush of adrenaline that keeps us addicted to the entire sales process. And honestly, it's the reason most salespeople are salespeople. If we weren't focused on competing, even if only within ourselves, we probably wouldn't be very successful at our jobs.

But when a female customer walks through the door, that competitive drive has to be refocused and redirected into a collaborative drive. Take it from me—as a salesperson I have learned to get an even bigger rush of adrenaline from collaborating with my clients and customers to reach a mutually satisfying outcome.

 Sales shouldn't be just about closing the deal—it should be about closing the *right* deal!

Playing a game and winning is all about ego. It takes a high level of self-confidence, even bravado, to spend one's life convincing others to pay money and make a purchase. There is no doubt that salespeople need a good amount of healthy ego to be successful, but sometimes our egos get out of hand and get us into trouble.

The best way to "win" when selling to a woman is to put your ego aside and work together to create a solution that works for her both now and in the long term. And the best way to do that is to stay out of the game—entirely. If it seems that she isn't very sure about the product or it doesn't really fit her needs, don't push it. Become her ally in the process. Be on *her* team, not on the opposing team. Right now you are probably grumbling that this approach certainly doesn't sound like a win—in fact, it sounds like you could lose the sale! Well, yes, you might. But the goodwill of doing what's best for her will earn you untold trust, respect, and probably a ton of referrals because you have done her a personal favor.

Let me share an example with you from something that recently happened to me during one of my sales calls. When clients call to book me as a speaker, they are interested in interviewing me to see whether I will be the right fit for their event. But I believe it is just as important for me to listen to their needs and make the same determination. I want to make sure that they are also the right fit for me.

 A successful salesperson knows his strengths and his weaknesses and is good at positioning himself in situations where his strengths shine.

I know from experience that my future as a professional speaker is best served when I am selective and make sure that I speak at events where my specific talents, topics, and delivery style place me in situations where I can be the most successful.

I recently had a female client call asking me to be her opening keynote at an upcoming event. She had not personally heard me speak but had heard good things from colleagues she respected. However, after a lengthy discussion, I began to realize that in this particular instance the audience would be better served by another type of speaker more qualified to speak on the specific issues their company was facing at that time. As a competitor, I had the deal closed. We had talked for a long time, gotten into our families and kids (as women do), and even discussed our last vacations. She was ready to hire me, and I could have done a good job for her—but I knew another speaker whose experience dealing with her company's very specific financial and economic issues would be exactly what she needed. Close the deal or walk away from the deal? Tough question.

I took myself out of competition mode and into collaboration mode and told her the truth: that as much as I wanted to take the job I felt that she had such specific economic and financial issues that I would rather refer her to an economist speaker I knew who could tackle her problems head-on with experience and clarity. The minute the words came out of my mouth, my competitive ego voice said, "That was stupid. You had everything but the contract signed and delivered!" But before these thoughts could resonate she said to me "I think in fourteen years of planning events I've never had a speaker turn down a job because he or she thought another speaker would be a better fit. I am amazed—and surprised. But most of all, I'm so thankful that you cared enough about me and my audience to think about what is best for us." And guess what? She hired me anyway. She hired us both. The other speaker did a fantastic opening that was right on the money (no pun intended), and I closed the event with a presentation that didn't compromise me or her audience. And remember how I said women were loyal to people they trust? She has referred me to more than ten other meeting planners and brought me back to her company on five different occasions. Word-of-mouth marketing at its best! All because I was willing to *not* close the deal. I positioned myself as her ally in her quest to find the right speaker, instead of as her competitor trying to "win" the game.

How about some more good news? The speaker that I referred them to was delighted that I had given him an opportunity to work with a new client and has since given my name to several of his clients as well. This was a win-win situation all around because I was willing to walk away from a done deal. Scary? Maybe. But absolutely necessary sometimes if your number one concern is to give your female customers the *best* service possible.

Deal Breaker #2

SHE DOESN'T THINK YOU VIEW HER AS A LEGITIMATE DECISION MAKER

QUIZ

Be honest!

1. A man and a woman walk into your place of business. They are obviously together. You walk up to them and the man steps forward and introduces himself. The woman has turned away and is looking at a brochure. What's your next move?

2. Have you ever asked the women in your life how they think you perceive their ability to make decisions, manage finances, or analyze information?

3. When you are working with a female customer, do you plan for the sales process to take longer than it typically does with male customers?

4. If you were the salesperson in the following scenarios, what would your expectations be (who is doing the buying, what are they shopping for, what kind of help will they need, and who else might be involved in the buying decision)?

    *   A woman who looks to be in her late sixties and a man in his twenties walk into a store that sells high-end stereo equipment.

    *   A professionally dressed woman wearing a wedding ring walks into an insurance agent's office and asks to speak with somebody about upgrading a life insurance policy.

    *   A man and woman walk onto the lot of a used car dealer and begin looking at pickup trucks.

5. When selling to women, what types of things do you do to let them know you respect them?

Every single woman I have ever spoken with regarding the buying process has had a horror story of being treated as an unintelligent, irresponsible, and financially inept decision maker from the moment they walked into a store or met with a salesperson. An assumption was made about her before she even spoke that was not only discourteous, but was also prejudiced and insulting. The truth about this deal breaker is simple: if you don't pass this test, chances are great that there will be no sale—ever!

From the moment a female customer enters your place of business, every action you take and every word you say must make it perfectly clear that you consider her to be a competent and independent decision maker capable of making a purchase without anyone else's help, advice, financial support, or input.

Is it *always* true that women are competent and independent decision makers? Of course not. But it's not always true of men either. The difference is that with men it is assumed to be true unless the man says or acts otherwise. He is given the benefit of the doubt. Women, on the other hand, often face salespeople who assume they are *not* the sole decision maker. A woman may be totally ignored when she enters a store. Or she may not be approached right away, with salespeople watching to see what she does instead. Women have even told me they have seen salespeople argue over who will "take this one" when they see a female customer walk in, each salesperson jockeying for the right to wait for the next man who walks in instead. Once approached, the insinuation often continues; women are often asked, "Are you sure you wouldn't like to discuss this with your husband?"—or partner, or dad, or boss. I doubt that many men are ever asked whether they'd like to talk over their purchase decision with someone else before they close the deal. I bet few men are ever asked questions such as "Do you want us to check your credit to make sure you can finance this?"

This happened to me when I was looking to rent new office space for my business. Although my husband was with me and we had discussed several options, I was the one making the final decision based on what was right for my situation and staff, and I explained this right up front to the leasing agent. Regardless, the agent continued to direct most of his information and questions to my husband, even though my husband would always direct them back over to me. I still hung in there (against my better judgment) because it was a good piece of property at a very good price. Finally he asked *us* for our credit and financial information. I again reminded him that I was the one who would be signing the lease. I gave him what he needed to check out my credit, but he just couldn't help himself and turned again to my husband and said, "Tell her that it's probably not a wise decision to exclude your income information. It is a prime location and the rent is fairly expensive, and by combining incomes I'm sure her credit number will be much higher." He wasn't even talking to me anymore—and he assumed my credit by itself would not be good enough to make the best financial deal. He didn't even check my credit first to see if this suggestion was warranted. Unfortunately (for the agent), I did not love the property, and now I was angry enough at him not to care *how* good a deal it was. I left and didn't lease anything from him at all.

It's not only unPROFESSIONAL to assume that a woman can't pay her own way, establish her own good credit, or take out her own loan, it's also PERSONALLY insulting. It would have been very easy for the leasing agent to have checked my credit and financial records and then, if he discovered that I was not qualified, come back with an alternative idea as to how we could fix the situation.

When in doubt, always assume she is a legitimate decision maker unless something happens to prove otherwise. This particular salesperson obviously did not know or take into consideration that two-thirds of all sales will be made or influenced by a woman on her own, by herself, without anyone else's help. So if the woman is doing most of the talking, if the person with her is referring the questions back to her, if she says she is the one doing the buying, and if she doesn't suggest to you that she needs help with the financing, then assume that she is willing and able to close the deal. Talk to *her*. Make eye contact with *her*. Get the credit information from *her*. Otherwise, you will lose the sale. If you ever, ever have any doubt about whether the woman in front of you is a legitimate decision maker, keep in mind that the odds are that she is. Those aren't odds you want to play around with.

I'm betting right about now that there are some of you reading this saying to yourself, "I don't have any issues selling to women. I'm not the type of person who stereotypes people. I don't carry around any preconceived notions or prejudices." The problem is that most of us, men and women, have some of these thoughts or behaviors that we simply are not aware of. You probably aren't as disrespectful as the leasing agent in my story, but women are masters at reading even the subtlest of clues or signs that you don't view them as legitimate decision makers.

The other thing to remember is that it isn't really important what you think you do or don't do anyway. The real questions are these: What does she think? How does she interpret your actions? What is her perception of your intent? If you have any negative feelings, assumptions, or attitudes—conscious or unconscious—about selling to a woman that might manifest themselves in some way through your behavior, tone of voice, or choice of words, then chances are good that she'll pick up on it pretty quickly. And this isn't just limited to salesmen. I've known plenty of saleswomen who heave just as big a sigh and disappear into the back room when a woman walks in.

Notice I'm saying *perceive, seem,* and *interpret,* not *know* or *prove in court.* Perception is the name of the game when it comes to communicating to a woman. It's not just what you say and do that counts. Women are exceptionally good at sensing and reading nonverbal clues, mainly because we're usually watching for them. Your female customer is listening to what you say, but she's even more attuned to what you don't say. She focuses on your tone of voice more than your words, and the look on your face more than your actions. If you are a person who is more literal than intuitive, you will probably find communicating with and selling to a female customer somewhat perplexing and will need to do a bit of extra work. Most of that work will have to be done before she even crosses your path. You must be brutally honest with yourself about any feelings you may have that could turn her off, or this deal breaker could trip you up every time.

One of the most accurate ways to assess this is for you to ask some women you know and trust to tell you how you come across to women. Do you appear angry when you really aren't? Do you get impatient when people don't get to the point quickly enough? Are you sarcastic—even if you say you're just kidding? Is there anything in your demeanor, style, or personality that women might read differently than what you intend? When it comes to this particular deal breaker, you need to make absolutely sure that it's not just your words but your entire manner that conveys respect. And that starts from within *long* before a word is spoken.

Why do so many people, men and women, automatically assume that they will have a better chance at making a sale or will make more money in a sale to a man than to a woman? For one thing, historically this has often been the case. In the past, men did make the majority of the purchases, earned more money, and as a result, had better lines of credit. However, today this is no longer true. And continuing to let past spending and buying patterns influence your sales approach in today's market could be devastating to your business. Some people justify avoiding female customers because they claim their personal experience shows that women are less likely to buy and less profitable to sell to when they do make a purchase. They have all kinds of stories about why women don't buy. Perhaps they ascribe behaviors to female customers based on what they've seen with the women in their own lives. One salesman's mother was indecisive and couldn't make a decision without asking his dad. A saleswoman had a sister who returned everything she bought, or she knew girls in high school who went to expensive boutiques and tried on everything in the store just to kill time and annoy the clerks.

But for every one of these scenarios, think of all the women who are totally the opposite. Women in *your* life who have great jobs and a sound financial future, independent women who have raised their kids and purchased homes, cars, and insurance—many without any help from anyone, and others with their husband's blessing either because he has figured out she is the better one to handle the money or he simply doesn't want to be bothered and is thrilled she's willing to take on the responsibility of handling their finances. And don't forget that 50 percent of all the women who come in to buy are single—they are totally independent and responsible for every purchase. This is a huge purchasing segment and one you do not want to miss out on.

Just remember, no matter what age she is, who she comes in with, or what she's looking at, odds are 2 out of 3 that she and she alone is ready and able to make a purchase on her own, with or without your help.

That being said, there are also those times when a woman who walks into your place of business may *not* be in a position to buy or even want to buy today. But there is certainly no guarantee that a man would buy today either. There are plenty of women (just like there are plenty of men) who are not ready or able to make a purchase when they walk into a store. Just think about this: with the amazing odds that a woman *will* buy 85 percent of the merchandise sold, your shot at making a sale is actually better when you're talking to a female than when you are talking to a man. That's certainly something to think about, isn't it?

The main problem with not giving a woman the benefit of the doubt is that, while a man may forgive you for assuming he's not ready or able to buy, underestimating a woman triggers a deep-seated response built up from many past encounters with dismissive salespeople. If a man is ignored when he walks in, he may not even notice unless he's really in a hurry. When he does need attention, he will have no problem getting it one way or the other. But the biggest difference is he won't take it personally, because it isn't part of a pattern. He will interpret it as a major deficiency in the salesperson. Of course, so will a woman, but in her mind the deficiency is PERSONAL and chances are she will assume it was intentional.

The bottom line is this: Treat each and every person as a potential legitimate decision maker and customer. That way, you can never go wrong.

Tip #1: Don't Make Assumptions Based on Who She's With

If a man and a woman walk in together, do not assume that the man is the buyer. This is a big mistake and creates a situation that is rarely salvageable. Recently, I was heading out to buy a new car. Although my husband and I always discuss major purchases, when it comes to cars we each pick out and buy our own. I was going to go alone, but at the last minute my husband decided to join me. I was totally prepared. I had done my research, knew exactly what I wanted, and was ready to buy if I found a good deal.

When we walked in, I immediately saw the exact car I was looking for right there on the showroom floor—the right color, the right make and model, the right extras. It even had the chrome wheels I had been debating getting—I wanted them, but they weren't a necessity and they were a bit expensive. I walked around to the driver's side (which should have been a good clue for the salesman), and my husband went to the passenger's side. It was a perfect moment until the salesman went right up to my husband without even looking in my direction and said, "Sir, what can I do to put you into this car today?"

At this point, my husband glanced at me and said, "There's nothing you can do for me, because this isn't going to be my car. And knowing my wife, there may not be a whole lot you're going to be able to do at this point to get her to buy from you either." He was so right. The salesman made a *big* mistake. He hadn't even considered that I might be the buyer. I wasn't even part of his equation. I hadn't even been included in a "What can I do to put you *both* into this car today?" In fact, when I tell this story to women, they immediately tell me a similar story and then get angry and say to me, "I hope you just walked right out of there and bought from someone else."

By addressing just my husband, the salesman certainly wasn't including me as PART OF THE PROCESS.

Remember, this deal breaker is usually not salvageable—many, if not most, women will walk away at this point. But I really, really liked this car and I was in a hurry and I didn't want to drive all the way across town to the other dealership. It also didn't strike me as an intentional sign of disrespect, and I could tell the salesman was embarrassed. So I waited to see what would happen next. This was one of those rare, wonderful moments where the salesman recovered quickly and graciously and did just the *right* thing. Without a moment's hesitation, he came around to my side, stuck out his hand and helped me out of the car, then said, "I apologize. Let's start over. My name is Jason and if you decide you would like to buy this car, I'd like to be the one to help you do that. And those chrome wheels you were admiring will be on me." Wow! I was impressed. He immediately recognized his mistake, worked to rectify it, and realized he had better quickly change my perception of him by recognizing me as the buyer *and* by adding something of value to go along with the apology.

Of course, men don't like to be slighted either, so when you're working with a couple, you need to be careful. Greet both people equally. Introduce yourself to both. At this point, remember either one or both could be making the purchase.

This tip also applies to assumptions you make about women with children, women who are with friends, or women on their own. Not only is half of the female purchasing population single but also, according to the Department of Health and Human Services, in 2002, 23 percent of all families with children were headed by single moms. Single moms will probably have their kids with them, and it may appear to be a bit chaotic, but that doesn't mean they aren't ready, willing, and able to buy—hopefully from you! Again, don't make any assumptions. It may be her elderly mom doing the buying or her twenty-year-old daughter. She may be doing the reconnaissance for her husband (I've done that a lot for my spouse), and he'll be the one to sign the contract, but he'll choose from the products and stores she has researched. So just how do you know who's doing the buying and who isn't? Give it a moment. Greet everyone, be friendly, make eye contact with everyone, and then just be patient. Women will let you know quickly enough who's doing the buying and who's just there for advice or support.

Tip #2: Don't Make Assumptions About Her Finances

In my car-buying experience, I fell victim to one kind of stereotyping—the idea that women don't buy manly things like cars (or computers, or flatscreen TVs, or life insurance policies, or lawn mowers, or trailer hitches). But sometimes salespeople discount a female buyer based on more than their perceptions of what women "should" be buying and what men "should" be buying. A common mistake salespeople make about a customer is to decide that she doesn't have the income, credit, or means by which to make a purchase based on her clothing or her bearing or just the fact that she is a woman walking in alone. Do not assume she can't afford your product or service by how she is dressed, what kind of car she drives, her appearance, or anything else other than the information she gives you. She may be dressed in a suit and heels, jeans, or workout clothes. She may look overwhelmed, confused, hurried, or stressed (and often all of the above). None of it matters when it comes to her ability to make a purchase.

Part of making an experience PRODUCTIVE for women buyers is understanding that they're buying on their time, not yours.

They may not have time to change clothes, drop the kids off, or study up on the product before they arrive. Women rarely have the luxury of making purchases when they are dressed to kill, have babysitters on call, and have lots of extra time off from work. That doesn't mean they don't have the money to spend with the right person.

Once I went with a friend of mine, an accountant, to help her buy appliances for her new house. We went to a store that was advertising one year of zero-interest financing, and that fit her budget needs perfectly. She found a salesman who was charming, professional, knew the products, listened to her needs, and then steered her in exactly the right direction for each item. In fact, he did everything perfectly—until the very end. The moment they sat down to sign the papers and discuss money, his tone changed. He began to talk more slowly, and then he leaned in toward her and said, "I will try to get through this finance stuff really quickly so I don't bore you. And I'll make it as simple as I can." Wow! All of a sudden she went from being a smart, respected consumer to a person who couldn't quite handle the difficult math involved in figuring out the price of the appliances with a one-year interest-free loan. It never even occurred to him that she knew more about finance and accounting than he ever would. And then he patted her (I am not kidding—it was a shoulder pat) and assured her that he would help her figure out a way to continue the financing beyond a year if she couldn't get it paid off in time.

So in a matter of seconds he undid all the POSITIVE feelings he'd built up initially and made her feel like a financial invalid. I can't imagine any salesperson reaching over and patting a man's shoulder and softly reassuring him that she would help him with the numbers so he could meet the payments. What was this salesperson's biggest problem? Faulty assumptions. I can assure you that he didn't earn any referrals from me or my friend.

Tip #3: Do Not Be Condescending or Patronizing

I know it may sound condescending and patronizing to even include this as a tip for what not to do. It doesn't seem like something anyone would have to be told to avoid. Unfortunately, we can often be *perceived* as condescending even when we think we are being very respectful. I do not mean that you would purposefully treat your customer as though she weren't smart or knowledgeable, but sometimes that could be how your presentation, tone of voice, expression, or demeanor might come across.

A detour into psychology can help explain why these lapses occur. Eric Berne's Transactional Analysis teaches us that when people talk they usually communicate from one of three points of view: the adult, the parent, or the child.

 The only healthy choice is to talk as an adult to someone you perceive to be an adult.

Condescending and patronizing communication occurs when we communicate with other adults from the role of the parent, talking to them the way we would talk to a child. The message we deliver can be critical or helpful, but the tone suggests that the person on the other end is not smart enough, capable enough, or intuitive enough to understand the message as we'd explain it to an adult.

You may be asking yourself, "What if my female customer really doesn't understand something I'm telling her?" The good news is, generally she will let you know. She will tell you to slow down or ask you to repeat some information. Another tip: Ask her! It might sound like this: "I don't know how much information you want or need. Do you want me to go into a lot of detail or just summarize the main points?" Also always tell her to let you know if she wants more or less information. (This is a good idea for both men and women. It keeps you from making wrong assumptions about either gender.)

Showing that you expect her to ask questions and giving informative, respectful answers means you're making her PART OF THE PROCESS and keeping things PRODUCTIVE—she doesn't have to listen to the parts she already understands. As far as asking questions goes, women don't have nearly the problem with asking for help and clarification that most men do. Women don't tend to see asking questions or admitting ignorance as a weakness. In fact, most women *hate* it when they don't understand something and almost always let you know to slow down, repeat what you said, or explain it differently—provided they think you will be responsive to that request and not annoyed or irritated.

Your reaction when a customer asks her first question is *very* important because it sets the stage for whether she will ask more questions or not.

Usually when she stops asking questions after only one, you've just hit trouble. If she asks more, it means she's comfortable in the situation and trusts you as a source of information—green light!

Now here's the tough part. Even though I stand by my statement that most women will let you know when they don't understand something, you do need to be aware that sometimes a woman indicates she doesn't understand by giving nonverbal clues instead of saying so outright. Guys don't generally give off a lot of nonverbal clues—they are much more likely just to tell someone what they want. Therefore, when selling to a woman, you *must* be tuned in to her facial expressions as well as her words.

The good news is women give really good, expressive, readable nonverbal clues.

If she looks confused, she probably is. If she looks overwhelmed by too much information, she probably is. And if she looks bored with your explanation, she probably is. In fact, a woman will usually *look* bored, annoyed, or exasperated before she verbalizes it. A really great salesperson will pick up her nonverbal messages before she even has to speak. Taking off her glasses and rubbing her eyes, heaving big sighs, rotating her neck around, biting her lip, frowning, shaking her head no—all good clues that she's got a problem with your presentation and it's best you take the time to check it out before pushing through.

You also have to be aware of the nonverbal signals *you're* sending. This means you have to be the picture of a PROFESSIONAL. As I mentioned before, women are paying close attention and will notice the slightest slip. Unfortunately, many women anticipate they will be treated in a disrespectful or patronizing manner because they have had past buying experiences where this happened. So be aware that your customer probably has her emotional antennae engaged, ready, and waiting for a signal from you to confirm what she is already expecting. Is this fair? Not at all. But it's reality.

From the moment the relationship takes off, a woman begins to sense how things are going to go if she continues to do business with you—your eye contact (or lack thereof), your handshake, your tone, your level of respect—she sees them and judges them all in an instant. When you first strike up a conversation, the odds might even be stacked against you depending on her past experiences and her degree of success with her buying relationships. But the good news is women are also very pleased and appreciative when they discover they have come across a salesperson who knows how to keep things POSITIVE, PRODUCTIVE, and PROFESSIONAL and treats them respectfully right from the start. Greet her. Look her in the eye. Smile and ask how you can help her. Then listen and use your experience and intuition to decide what to do next. If you can do that, you're a long way toward making a deal and developing a long-lasting customer.

Deal Breaker #3

SHE DOESN'T LIKE YOU

QUIZ

Be honest!

1. If you were your own customer, would you find the sales environment welcoming? Intimidating? Confusing? How would the women in your life that you respect describe your sales environment? Have you ever asked them?

2. What are five character traits that make you a good salesperson? What are five traits that you believe limit your sales potential when selling to a woman?

3. What do the women in your life say about your communication style? Your personality? Do you get along better with men than women? If so, think about why that is the case.

4. What are three types of customers with whom you really don't like working? Who are your favorite customers? Would you rather work with men or with women? Why?

5. What do you think your female friends like most about you? Which of those traits can you integrate into your sales style when selling to female customers?

Most men (and a few women) are surprised to learn that not liking a salesperson is near the top of a woman's list of deal breakers. In fact, men that I've spoken with have said, "If I had to *like* everybody I bought from, I wouldn't own half of what I have. I don't have to like somebody to recognize a good deal when I see one!" Ah, those results-driven men. Women, on the other hand, are looking for a buying experience where there is a PERSONAL connection and business is handled in a POSITIVE and PRODUCTIVE manner. They will find it hard to feel comfortable dealing with somebody they don't like. For women, it's not just about whether you can do what they need done or offer the product or service they need or want at the time. It's also all wrapped up in whether they will enjoy going through the experience with you.

The hardest thing about avoiding this deal breaker is that egos can often get in the way when we try to take a closer look and evaluate how some of our own individual personality traits come across to others. Don't get me wrong—ego is very important in sales, especially when it supports the confidence and positive attitude needed to negotiate and close a deal. Healthy ego is also a major part of our confidence and self-esteem—both of which play a significant role in any successful sales situation.

But ego becomes a stumbling block to improvement when it keeps us from taking a realistic look at how our interpersonal skills, our attitudes, our behaviors and actions, and our style of communicating affects other people. Nothing you say or do will be interpreted or perceived the same way by everyone—if it did, you wouldn't need this book! The traits and habits some people like about us are exactly the things that turn others away. A successful salesperson develops a gut, intuitive sense about when to engage certain behaviors and when to keep them out of the process. And it can change with each customer. Most people want to be liked— but salespeople *really, really* want to be liked. Let's face it—it's one of the perks of the job, one of the highs, one of the reasons why we went into the business—so people could reinforce and validate that they liked us enough to buy from us. That's why we usually take it personally when someone doesn't close and commit to us. Rejection is one of salespeople's biggest fears. But there's good and bad news about this whole rejection thing: the good news is that sometimes it has nothing to do with you—they just didn't want the product or found a better deal or decided to buy later. The bad news is sometimes it *is* you and you alone that turned them away. Something about you just didn't do it for them.

 As the book says—maybe the potential customer is "just not that into you."

The secret to being a great salesperson, however, is that you totally understand that sometimes it *is* just about you—and instead of blaming the customer, the economy, the prices, or the product—you accept responsibility for figuring out what you can do or change in yourself and your selling style that will work better the next time. I have coached and counseled many salespeople who complain, "I just can't stand rejection." My response is, "No, you don't like the thought that perhaps someone didn't want to buy from you, but what you really can't stand is the realization that you might have to take a brutally close look at yourself and figure out what and why you are doing what you do and what you have to change."

Some people I've offered this advice worry that changing the way they present themselves to their customers will make them seem phony or false, or that they'll be compromising their values.

Now I'm not suggesting that you behave in a manner that is contradictory to who you are or what you believe. That *is* phony and misleading, and in plain language, unethical. But rarely have I found that changing the traits that make you harder to like will compromise your values at all. In fact, these are generally behaviors that do just the opposite—they *take away* from who you really are. They are usually behaviors that you have adopted over the years to compensate for the things you want and don't quite know how to get in more acceptable ways.

I remember counseling a woman we will call Laura. She started coming to me right after divorcing her first husband. All she could talk about was her husband—what he had done, what he hadn't done, how he had made her miserable. When I tried to turn it around and talk about her, she would say, "Oh, this isn't about me—I'll be fine now that he's gone." Nothing I could say would convince her that perhaps, just perhaps, she had played an equal part in the breakup. But after three years in her second marriage, she was in trouble again and came back to see me. But this time, there was a distinct difference that gave me hope that perhaps we could save this marriage. The first day she walked into my office, she stated simply, "I guess it's me." "So how did you come to that conclusion?" I asked. "Well," she said, "My ex-husband used to say that I didn't act like I cared about him and that I never told him what I felt unless I was mad. I was so angry with him that I just ignored what he said and figured it was his fault that I didn't care or communicate. Well, my current husband—who I love to death and would do anything for—just said the *exact* same thing to me. Same words, same tone. And he is a totally different person than my first husband. So I guess when two very different people tell you the exact same thing about yourself—then there must be some truth to it."

Even though this is a story about a personal relationship, the same lesson holds true for any relationship—especially sales, where liking and trusting someone is so crucial, at least for women. Exactly what makes us like or dislike other people is difficult for most of us to put into words. It's a combination of all sorts of things wrapped up in a bit of intuition and gut feeling and then filtered through our past history with people and situations. And there is certainly truth to the saying "You can't please everyone." There are definitely times when the reason someone doesn't like you has absolutely nothing to do with you and everything to do with the other person. But we can't use those times to excuse ourselves from doing the best we can to explore and change the things about us that really do irritate, annoy, and frustrate other people.

To be successful in sales you *must* be aware of the things you do and say that might not be appealing to other people. Then you *must* be willing to change those things.

In the effort to be your best in any interaction with a potential client, you have to be flexible: If something you're doing doesn't seem to be working, stop doing it and try something else, right away. It's PERSONAL, not logical, the things that make some people like us and others dislike us. That said, you need to understand up front what types of behavior will likely turn a woman away from the start, because women make decisions about your likability very quickly. So a woman's first impression of you is unbelievably important. Let's take a look at how you can make the very best first impression.

Tip #1: Be Genuinely Friendly

"Duh," you are probably thinking. "I thought we were going to learn some new ideas. Being friendly is so obvious. I can't learn anything new about that." Wrong! For a woman, friendliness goes beyond a smiling face. It goes beyond just being a nice person. It goes beyond courtesy. It is a whole package of comfort, concern, communication, and most important, connection. Because as much as a woman needs to like you, she also wants you to like her. These are very intertwined for a woman. And it makes total sense. How can we like someone if they don't like us as well?

 Liking and being liked are all wrapped up in one package for a woman.

Women view appropriate friendliness as the first step toward building this two-way PERSONAL connection. Read this as "If you are being sincerely friendly to me, I will probably like you, and as a bonus, you will probably like me as well!" Often the men I talk to mistakenly assume that a woman's desire to be liked stems from an insecurity, while they act like they don't care whether people like them or not. Well, neither of those ideas is quite accurate. Most women like to be liked, not because they are insecure, but simply because it's just more fun and comfortable going through life being liked than not—one less thing to have to worry about. Women understand that when they are with someone who likes them, they can let their guard down and just be themselves. And as a result, they can accomplish quite a bit more. Most men feel exactly the same way but won't admit it. Come on . . . guys like to be liked, too. It makes life a lot easier.

In a sales relationship, both liking you and being liked by you can affect her decision whether to buy from you or not. Men are a bit different—they will often buy from someone they don't like if they have any indication that they can still get the results they want. They just write the salesperson off as a pain in the neck and are even more determined to get the best deal possible. It brings out their competitive spirit: when a man doesn't like someone, he moves in, becomes more aggressive, and tries even harder to win. When a woman doesn't like someone, she is more apt to move away—away from the confrontation and unpleasantness—to do her business elsewhere.

Man or woman, you might also be thinking, "What does being friendly have to do with whether I like somebody or not? Maybe I like her fine, but I'm just having a bad day. Why take things so PERSONALLY?" There's that all-important word again: PERSONAL. All I can say is that most women will perceive any gesture, comment, or behavior that they view as "unfriendly" as a sign that the other person does not like them, and they *will* take it personally. Therefore, scoring high on the friendliness scale is much more important when you are selling to a woman than to a man. (In fact, some men even get weird about a salesperson, man or woman, they think is "too friendly"—some men view it as *too* personal or even as an invasion of their privacy. They want to just concentrate on the business at hand.)

The nice thing about being around a salesperson who is friendly is that it makes the whole experience seem so much easier and more enjoyable—and it certainly puts you in a better buying frame of mind. You feel like this person truly wants to help you, a rare feeling in our crazy world. Friendliness brings POSITIVE feelings to the surface, and that means the way is clear to make a purchase.

A woman is always on the lookout for a salesperson who can create a sense of calmness and comfort.

When I was interviewing companies to build our new swimming pool, I looked at several criteria. Of course, there was price and quality and reputation. But once I narrowed it down to two companies who had all those attributes, I went with the contractor who had the friendliest and calmest demeanor. The other guy was grumpy and stressful to be around for more than even a few minutes. He didn't act like he liked anything: himself, me, or the job. And since I would be the one home the most while it was being built, I couldn't imagine working with him day after day. His pools looked awesome, his price was even a bit lower. But I simply didn't *like* him. Now, I admit it took me awhile to convince my husband. He initially went for the lower-price contractor and felt that my "I don't like him" reason was ridiculous, but after a couple more meetings, he had had enough of the guy's grouchy attitude himself.

So what makes you friendly? Well, smiling doesn't hurt, especially when you're first meeting your customer. But friendly goes way beyond a pleasant, smiling demeanor. Here is my definition:

Friendly is giving genuine attention by sharing both your time and your energy with a positive, helpful attitude.

You have allotted the "time" necessary to listen and converse without being distracted, and you exert the "energy" required to show that you are committed to the conversation through your gestures, facial expressions, and dialogue. *Friendly* means that you show due consideration and pay close attention to what is going on throughout the sales process and you make it a pleasant, comfortable environment in which to do business. Friendly is not just about you—friendly people show a definite and sincere concern for others and have a wonderful way of making others feel validated, included, and important. To be perceived as friendly it is important that you pay very close attention to her expressions, her confidence level, her communication style, her sense of humor, and her mood—and try to match your behavior to hers without compromising your own unique personality. Don't be either timid or overbearing. Friendly does not ever fall into the "extremes" of communication. It plays the best right in the middle zone of comfort and acceptance. It doesn't feel forced or phony.

One lesson that I learned the hard way is that it's not just *un*friendliness that can foul up the sale. Inattention or distraction can be just as detrimental. Not so long ago, I was delivering an after-dinner presentation to a large corporate group. I had been seated at dinner next to one of the event planners. Although I was friendly to her throughout the dinner, I was also concentrating on my upcoming presentation. When I was done giving the speech, I felt I had done a great job: I included everything they asked for and more, and I got a standing ovation.

Now, like you, I love repeat business. In fact, I had told the planners I had part two of the speech all thought out, and this particular event planner had been very excited about bringing me back. So a couple of days after the presentation I emailed her asking for an appointment to discuss what our next steps would be. No response. I followed up, but I never heard back. What had

I done or not done to squelch the opportunity I thought was a done deal?

Finally, I got in touch with someone on the committee who liked me enough to tell me what was going on. Basically, I had committed a major deal breaker—the event planner had told the committee that I had been very unfriendly during dinner. In other words, she didn't feel I had given her my full and deserved attention in terms of time and energy—and she was right—I hadn't. Fortunately, because I was able to track down the problem, I was able to recover the sale. I called her and left a voice message to get as PERSONAL as I could. I told her that I was sorry that I had not been able to spend more time with her at the dinner before my presentation, but that I was focusing entirely on what I was going to say. I told her that because I enjoyed working with her and valued our relationship, I had felt especially responsible for making sure I included everything she had requested. Then I concluded with, "When I come back to do part two, I would like to carve out some time for you and me to have a drink or coffee because I would enjoy getting to know you better." She called back the next day and began by saying, "Connie, I thought you were mad at me. We had always had so much fun together and I was looking forward to having dinner with you. In fact, I was the one who made sure I was going to be seated right next to you, but you seemed distracted. I should have known it was because you were thinking about your presentation." *I* should have known better than to think that being friendly without giving her my full time and energy was good enough.

 Remember, your time and energy are what she wants, expects, and deserves from you during the sales process.

Now, some salespeople lean too far in the opposite direction. They come across as phony. Phoniness is a big turnoff, especially for women, who will feel nervous because they don't know what you're really like. If you're not presenting your real self, she can't form a PERSONAL connection with you. She can't feel like she's PART OF THE PROCESS because you're playing a whole different kind of game. And she won't feel very PRODUCTIVE because she'll be thinking about what's going on with you instead of concentrating on what she needs and how you can get it to her.

These days, most people know you have to be genuine if you want to get anywhere. However, it is impossible for any of us to be happy, content, and satisfied all the time. We are going to have terrible days, personal problems, aches and pains, and life struggles. But throughout all of those, we can still *genuinely* believe that our customers deserve to have the best possible service from us. And we can still make the choice to treat them positively, regardless of what's going on in our own worlds. Choosing to treat a customer well instead of badly is always the right choice—even if it's not exactly how you are *really* feeling at that moment. There's nothing phony about that!

However, if it comes to a point where you are having to act more upbeat than you are genuinely feeling, then it's time to take a look at what's going on in your life. Genuine and happy usually go together, along with content, comfortable, and pleasant. If these are things you aren't experiencing in your life, then sales won't be an easy place for you to fulfill your career dreams.

 The very best salespeople truly enjoy their life, their job, and the joy of helping others find what they need.

Being genuinely friendly isn't surface. It is PERSONAL and POSITIVE; it comes from within you. It means you like your life and your job. You are generous with your time and open with your ideas. You are polite and respectful. You truly like what you are doing, you respect the product and service you represent, and you're delighted to have the chance to share it with her. In other words, from a woman's perspective, you are someone real who would make a good partner in her search for whatever she needs. She determines that you are someone she would *like* to do business with.

The bottom line, for a woman, is that friendliness is more than courtesy or a pleasant demeanor. *Friendly* means someone she likes—and someone she wants to do business with.

Tip #2: Earn Her Respect

There are two ways you can earn a customer's respect. One is to be respected for what you do, your expertise, education, and credentials. Your knowledge of the product or service shines through and you have earned the right to be treated as an "expert" who can help your customer make good decisions that will have a positive impact. The second is the respect you receive for being a good, decent, trustworthy person who models healthy, assertive behavior. "Aren't they both one and the same?" you might ask. No way. I may think you are a good, trustworthy person, but you aren't necessarily the one I want to design my new home or install my new sound system. Or I can respect your skills, talent, and expertise and still not trust that you will have my best interests in mind or stand by your product in the long term.

To a woman, like and respect are a package deal.

When I talk to men about how women want to like their sales reps and be liked in return, they usually scoff and say, "The *only* thing I care about is respect." But some men have admitted to me that they might even throw respect out the window if it meant they could still get the end result they were going after—what they wanted at the right price.

You will rarely hear a woman say something like that! Most women don't separate "like" from "respect" the way men can and do. I believe this is because men and women often have different relationships with the term *respect*. Men can respect someone because he is powerful or athletic or intelligent or wealthy, even if they don't like him. They can like someone who is fun or easy to be with without necessarily respecting who he is or what he does. Women, on the other hand, tend to respect and like someone for the same reasons: they think he is a good person who can be trusted and they feel good when they are with him. Sometimes, women may "respect" someone's position, or his age, or his credentials enough to listen, learn, and be courteous, even if they dislike him. They may even do business with someone they don't respect (or don't like) on occasion—if they *have* to—but it doesn't mean they would choose to do business with that person again if given the choice. And they won't hesitate to tell others *not* to use that salesperson.

When we first moved to Dallas, I was interviewing a new CPA to handle my business finances. (Remember, every time you are interviewing with someone, you are selling yourself.) The first woman I interviewed appeared very knowledgeable (PROFESSIONAL) and I was drawn to her personality right away. In fact, I was thinking how lucky I was to have met someone I enjoyed so much in such a short amount of time. We even discussed going to lunch after the meeting. She asked the right questions, making me PART OF THE PROCESS. Everything was perfect and I was just about to say, "You're hired," when she told me that I would be glad to know that she had a few little "tricks" in terms of doing my taxes that would save me a lot of money. Really? Now she definitely had my interest. I would love to save money on taxes as much as the next person. But when I asked for some examples, she was vague and said, "Oh, you just leave that to me. I have my ways. Just know that you will be delighted with the outcome." Suddenly I was a bit wary, so I asked with a laugh, "It's all legal, right?" Her answer? "Well, mostly." Then she told me that her fees were a bit higher, but the savings I would get would more than make up for it. In other words, I was being told I could pay her to cheat on my taxes. I stopped liking and respecting her at the very same moment. I was angry at her suggestion, insulted at her insinuation, and perplexed that she felt a need to resort to those tactics to get business.

 As salespeople, our character—the essence of who we are and what we stand for—is present in every transaction.

The moment we lose respect for ourselves and resort to any tactics that are illegal, unethical, or just plain wrong—our customers will never forget us. And most women will never forgive you because they will take it PERSONALLY. So how do you earn—and keep—your customer's respect? Do the right thing at all times. Be honest. Be genuine. You can never go wrong when you do what is right.

Tip #3: Keep Your Complaints to Yourself

Complaining sends a clear message: you don't like something, you're angry or upset about it, and you have made a choice to share those negative feelings with someone who probably didn't ask or want to hear about it. It's not at all what a female customer wants. She will *never* enjoy listening to your complaints—even if you have a reason to, even if you have a right to, even if she seems like she will understand, even if it would make you feel better, and even if she starts it.

Often salespeople say to me, "Connie, I can't imagine ever complaining in front of a customer. Who would do this?" Well, it happens all the time. You may not even realize you're doing it. You may be on the phone and she can overhear your conversation—you aren't complaining directly *to* her, but she's drawn into the negativity. You're having a discussion with a coworker and it moves into gripes about workload, stressful changes, late deliveries, or service problems. Or maybe she asks about the availability of a product and you respond by complaining about the lack of inventory or manufacturing problems. The phones keep ringing and you complain that the office assistant is never at her desk. And the list goes on.

Anytime you are blaming something or someone else during the sales process, she will hear it as complaining.

You are also letting her know that you don't have a lot of control when it comes to seeing this sale through to the end—there are tons of things out of your hands. True or not, it isn't what a woman wants to hear. She wants to feel that you can handle this and take care of any problems that arise without involving her.

 Women tend to be worriers—don't get her started worrying about your ability to do whatever is necessary to make this a positive and productive experience.

You need to be honest about inventory, schedules, and delivery dates, but you don't have to complain and blame at the same time. She has to respect you, your company, and your product in order to feel comfortable closing the deal. Making this a POSITIVE experience for her begins with you. Keep your complaints and gripes to yourself and you will have a far better chance of closing the deal.

"Doesn't complaining bother men, too?" you might ask. To be honest, it doesn't, not nearly as much as it does women. Men tend to just join in on the grumbling. Observe a group of guys when you have a chance. A little bit of mutual "Can you believe the stock market?" or "How about the price of gas!" seems to make a guy feel closer to the salesperson, like they now have something in common. And men tend to be focused on getting the deal done as fast as possible, so they know they aren't going to have to put up with you for long. But women are focused on how the experience feels, and if you're complaining, they can instantly visualize how working with you in the future is going to look—and it doesn't look good.

Another thing to keep in mind is that most women spend a great deal of time dealing with, worrying about, thinking of, and caring for others. Even when they're not directly engaged in caretaking activities, the people they care about are on their minds. And many of those people are grumpy, moody, manipulative, or going through some rough patch or another. Psychologically, many women have a powerful capacity for recognizing when someone is in trouble and an insatiable desire to step in to "fix it" or somehow help. And, believe me, it's exhausting work to take on responsibility for someone else's happiness. (I always tell women that they are responsible *to* other people, not *for* other people—but they don't always listen.) So the second you start complaining, her instinctive response will likely be, "Great, one more person I've got to take care of." Her natural inclination will be to listen and try and solve your problem, offer some advice, help you get help, and work hard to make you a happier person. And when a woman moves into the "therapist/mother" role, she will move out of the mood to buy!

The sales process should be one of the rare areas in a woman's life that is totally about her—not about someone else. She shouldn't ever have to be subjected to your negativity. (Of course, she's also capable of being the difficult one at times, but you're not *her* customer.)

The shopping experience for her needs to be as PERSONAL and POSITIVE as possible, and that starts with you and your attitude.

One rainy day, I walked into a plant nursery and was greeted by a salesperson who immediately said to me, "Don't you absolutely hate days like this?" As a matter of fact, I don't hate rainy days, but

I suddenly hated the fact I had possibly ruined what had so far been a good day by stopping into this particular store. But then I heard whistling. I followed it and found another salesperson looking over the new flowers that had just arrived. He stood amid an array of colors and fragrances and looked up at me, smiled, and said, "A little rain was all they needed—look how gorgeous the flowers are now!" Gee, I wonder which person I chose to do business with. What a difference an attitude makes. Each salesperson only uttered one sentence, but what powerful sentences they were. Same rainy day—but one looked at it with disdain and the other looked at it with a sense of joy. And guess who wrote up the order for three hundred dollars in plants, flowers, and trees?

Now some of you may be using an old excuse: "If I tried to act like everything is perfect all the time, it would be phony." Not true. Studies show that people who are angry, upset, or sad can do a lot to change those feelings simply by *acting* like they are content and happy for a while. Just try smiling, tell a funny story instead of sharing a bad experience, say something positive instead of something negative, think about what makes you feel good rather than focusing on what makes you feel bad, compliment instead of criticize, and forgive instead of holding a grudge—just for a little bit. And you will be amazed. Those blame and complain tendencies will fly out the window.

Yes, we all have bad days. We all feel crummy some times. We all have personality traits that might turn some people off. We all have things going on in our personal lives that are sad, frustrating, and difficult. We all have worries and disappointments. But life is about choices.

> Much of life is out of our control, but we can always choose how to behave, how to act, and how to treat other people.

The key is to view the bad things that happen in your life as less important to who you are than how you choose to react to and deal with those situations. And if you can always make the effort to treat people respectfully and behave graciously even in the worst of times—you will be a much better person. Believe me when I say that women will pick up on your positive attitude, your commitment, your ability to enjoy yourself and your job, and probably decide that you are just the one whom they want to have a business relationship with.

Deal Breaker #4

SHE DOESN'T TRUST YOU

QUIZ

Be honest!

1. Think about the last three sales you closed with women. How did you present information during those sales?

    - Did you give only information that they asked you for?
    - Did you offer any information that could be seen as negative without being asked?
    - Were you clear and explicit about all elements of financing?

    Now answer the same questions about the last three sales you closed with men. Are your answers different?

2. Do you think the women in your life would describe you as a trustworthy person? Do you interact with your female customers in the same way you interact with the other women in your life in terms of being honest, forthright, and respectful?

3. Consider your last five sales that involved selling products or services that the customer was not originally shopping for. How many of those sales were to women? How did you sell those other products and services to your female customers? Do you think that those extra items were always smart buying decisions?

4. Do you think your sales approach changes at the end of a month or quarter (when you're trying to meet your quota or earn a bigger bonus)? Are you more interested in selling to men or women at those times?

Trust—one of the most important elements in every relationship, personal or professional. So you might ask why it isn't the first deal breaker. One e-mail I received read, "What good does it do to like someone or even respect someone if you can't trust them?" Another said it even better, "If you don't trust someone, you wouldn't like or respect them to begin with." I totally agree—in order of importance, trust should really be #1. But I listed the deal breakers in the order in which you are likely to break them. You can be a game player or set up a competitive sales atmosphere with the first words out of your mouth. A woman can tell right away if you view her as a legitimate decision maker. Within minutes she'll begin to judge whether you are a friendly and genuinely likable person. But for her to determine whether or not she can trust you or not will take more time.

Although trust is critical in the grand scheme of things, you will have to make it through the other deal breakers to even have the chance to prove that you are a trustworthy person.

One of the biggest problems many salespeople (especially those who have been in the business a long time) have with the issue of trust is that they expect to fall back on their reputations and past histories of being an honest person and don't really feel the need to have to prove themselves over and over. The truth is, that's exactly what salespeople have to do, day after day, time after time. This is where ego can get in the way again. You may know you are a person with high values and integrity, and you may have shown that to people again and again through your past actions, behaviors, and commitments, but each new client presents a fresh slate. Here is a person who may know little to nothing about you; trust has to be developed and proven to every single person, every single time, and during every single transaction. Even with a repeat customer who has had a good experience with you, you cannot become complacent and stop working to keep the trust alive. The problem with trust is that it is very hard to build and amazingly easy to destroy, so one misstep on this front could cost you the customer and the sale.

At this point, some of you may be wondering why this is a specific deal breaker for a woman. Isn't trust important for a man, too? Indeed, trust *is* important for a man, but there are some distinct differences between how men and women define trust and integrate trust into the buying process.

First, let's look at how men and women determine from the get-go whether a person is trustworthy. Men tend to gauge whether they can trust the salesperson to do what they need done, looking at red flags in context of the results. Can he get what he wants and needs, at the agreed-upon price, on time? If so, then the salesperson seems pretty trustworthy to him. Women, on the other hand, are looking at the experience more holistically (you've heard this before). They observe and pay attention to tones of voice and nonverbal clues (like not making eye contact or talking too fast or too much) to get an idea whether the salesperson is all-around trustworthy. Men focus more on the one-on-one relationship— "Can I trust him to deal with *me* at this moment for this particular transaction?" A man has said to me, "Sure, I would prefer to work with someone I trust completely, but that's not always possible. So for the ones I can't trust, I just figure out how to stay one step ahead of the game. They soon learn to not mess with me." Another man said, "I learn quickly what I can trust them to do and what I can't, and I go from there." So one difference between men and women in this area of trust is that men seem more willing than women to continue to do business with someone they might not believe in or trust completely, giving the reason that they're confident they can handle the situation. Men tend to believe they will be able to weed out the truth from nontruth and still end up with a good deal.

Women don't quite see it that way. With women, it's not about whether we can handle any attempts to cheat us or not, it's about avoiding the situation altogether. We don't want to be on our guard all the time. We need to believe full-on that you will do right by us so we don't have to spend the time, energy, or emotion to be on edge throughout the process trying to figure out what's real and what's not.

Women often look beyond just how they are being treated or handled at that moment and take the whole picture into consideration to determine trustworthiness. A perfect example is what happened one day when I was shopping for a jacket in a department store. I found one I loved, but they didn't have my size. I went up to the counter to ask the salesperson to check in the back to see if they had more in stock when I noticed the jacket I was looking for hanging under plastic next to the cashier. When I went over to look at it, the salesperson ripped the plastic away along with a note that said "Marilyn 6:00 pm" and announced, "Here is just the size you need." Now, I've shopped enough to know that this jacket had been placed on hold by Marilyn—I have done that many times myself. So I said to the saleswoman, "What about Marilyn? Doesn't she have until six to pick it up? It's only noon." "Oh, well," she said, "next time she won't forget her credit card." After thinking about it I decided I just couldn't buy it—at that moment. I did find another salesperson, pointed out the coat on hold, gave her my name and phone number, and told her if Marilyn hadn't picked it up by six o'clock to give me a call; I'd come right over and buy it from her. Why? Because I didn't like, respect, or *trust* the original salesperson. I didn't want her to get any part of a commission from me.

I was putting myself in Marilyn's shoes and thinking not only how she would feel, but how I would feel if it were me. I couldn't PERSONALLY connect to the saleswoman and, although she was trying to make my trip PRODUCTIVE, it was at the cost of her professionalism.

One reason women and men react so differently to trust issues is that, while many men seem to have the "don't trust anyone until they prove you different" approach, women are much more likely to give someone the benefit of the doubt. When a man walks into most negotiating situations, he *expects* someone to try to take advantage of him. For him, it's simply part of the process. So he's prepared to not trust anything or anyone—and is often proven right. However, when a woman walks in, she expects the exact opposite. Although women are not naïve enough to believe that all people are honest and trustworthy, most certainly don't want to believe that's the norm.

Women are much more disappointed and take it much more PERSONALLY when they find themselves dealing with someone who doesn't appear to be reliable and truthful.

As a result, the framework of trust is very fragile for a woman. It may take quite a while for her to move from giving you the benefit of the doubt into handing over her trust, but it takes only seconds to destroy her faith in you. So when you are selling to a woman, you have to do more than just *be* trustworthy. You have to *prove* that you're trustworthy—over and over at every step of the transaction. Say what you mean and mean what you say.

Some things in life are just out of our control. But not when it comes to our self-respect and our conscious decision to be a trust-worthy person. We *always* have the choice to be a good, decent, respectful, and honest person. We always have the choice to be someone that others can count on and trust to do what we say we will without games, deceit, or manipulation.

And let's face it, in the world of sales, reputation is every-thing—and it begins and ends with trust.

Tip #1: Always Tell the Truth

This one is obvious, of course, but, unfortunately, it comes up a lot in sales. In fact, I've had salespeople tell me, "If I really told the truth—the *whole* truth—I'd never make a sale." I tell them, "Then you better switch companies or products or both. If the only way you can sell someone on your ideas, products, or services is to lie, then something is very wrong." Sometimes the boundary between positioning your product to show it off at its best and hiding its flaws or exaggerating its capabilities seems to get a little thin. As tempting as it may be to say whatever is necessary to make the sale, it's also deceitful.

As a professional speaker, I have a lot of friends who are also in the same business. Believe me, we all have a few bad memories or regrets about times in the beginning of our careers when we would agree to speak to almost *any* group, *anywhere*, about *anything*— even if it was a topic or subject that wasn't really in our area of expertise—because we didn't want to lose the sale. The nice term for this is "giving the customer what they want," but the truth is that it's not being totally honest with our client or ourselves about what we can or cannot do to deliver the very best results. Then we would find ourselves smack in front of several hundred people with a speech that wasn't bad, but it certainly wasn't the caliber that our audience deserved. And the evaluations usually showed it.

There was one event in my first year of speaking that, unfortunately and fortunately, I will never forget. Unfortunately, because I could have done a much better job, and fortunately, because it was a lesson that I will always remember. I had been asked to keynote a large sales conference. The company had experienced a very difficult year and sales were down, quotas had not been reached, bonuses and commissions were slashed, and the company was in the process of reorganizing and cutting some jobs. They wanted me to challenge their audience to rise above this economic slump and also to teach some new sales techniques and strategies that even the most experienced salesperson could use in their changing environment. This kind of presentation was right up my alley, so they offered me the job. Deal closed—perfect day! Until they began to discuss logistics. They told me that my speaking time slot was 9:00 to 10:00 pm, *after* a reception with an open bar, *after* a five-course dinner, *after* a rather lengthy awards ceremony. Now I can certainly entertain and motivate an after-dinner crowd, and I can teach some hard-hitting, results-oriented strategies to help salespeople. But these are usually two very different presentations. I knew without a doubt that this was not the right time slot for the kind of presentation they wanted, but I didn't say a word. I did what salespeople often do—I decided I would just figure out "how to make it work." That evening at 9:45 (a bit later than planned, of course) I found myself looking out on a sea of very tired, extremely full, and rather tipsy faces, and I knew I had done both my client and myself a disservice by not being honest. I did make it work—sort of. My presentation was okay. But we can't afford to just be okay.

We have to be amazing, memorable, and right-on-target in order to survive and be successful in sales.

Since then, I have never allowed a client or myself to put my presentation in the wrong time slot. I convince them either to change the presentation topic to fit the time slot or put the presentation in a different spot. I become a consultant who cares enough to tell them the truth about what will work and what won't. If they want solid, challenging information I "sell" them on the fact that it has to be delivered to an open, awake, sober, and eager audience during the day, or I "sell" them an entertaining and motivating presentation after dinner. I learned a valuable lesson: Be up front and honest—resist the temptation to close the deal you know is not in the best interest of yourself or your customer.

 You are a consultant, an educator, a mentor, and a planner—you are being counted on to share all your knowledge and expertise to make sure your customers make the best choice possible.

Selling, as we discussed before, is about knowing yourself really, really well so your customer can be comfortable knowing that you have their back. If we aren't honest up front, our customers—especially the women—will figure it out quickly.

I often find that some people have a hard time distinguishing between lying and exaggerating or stretching the truth. Most successful salespeople are usually great storytellers who can add humor, depth, and interest to ordinary and mundane events. What happens in real life and the stories they tell about it later are often quite far apart. When asked, they will say, "Oh, it wouldn't be funny if I told the real story." And that storytelling ability can be a great advantage when used to engage and entertain people. But you have to be very careful about bringing this trait or skill into the sales process. A woman might find it interesting to hear a story that is animated and fun, but she will not find it entertaining at all when she wants and needs honest, accurate information about something she is about to buy. If your product is a good one, then it can stand on its own without your attempt to make it sound better than it is. If it can't, then maybe it's time to find something else to sell. Tell all the stories you want about the product, other customers who loved the product, how the product was developed, or how the product has been improved—just make sure they are true. Resorting to exaggeration or deceit will *not* help you close the deal with a woman, but it will prove to her that your word is not to be trusted.

Tip #2: Don't Make Her Hunt for Information

There is another component to the less than truthful scenario, and that is using the tactic of omission in order to sell—eliminating or not explaining information that you are afraid might ruin the deal. While some people will say omitting information is not lying, they are only fooling themselves. Omitting anything that a customer needs to know in order to make a fair, qualified decision *is* lying. The interview process is a perfect example. What a person omits from her resume can be very misleading and even damaging to a company who hires her, and is often more important information than what one can see in print.

The key advantage of selling to women is their loyalty and the positive word of mouth they share that can work to your advantage. The best way to achieve this is to make sure they make a purchasing decision they are happy with in the long term. The product she buys has to fit in with her life outside the store. That is why women have a higher return rate than men. I always tell commissioned salespeople not to spend the commission they make for a couple of weeks—if they sold to a woman. Because it's not really a final sale just because a woman has paid and left with the merchandise. Many women will wait and make their final decision when they get home or to the office. How does it fit, wear, look, feel, ride, taste, sound? Is it as useful, fun, dependable, convenient, time-saving, or reliable as she thought it was going to be?

It will be bad news for you if she discovers any "hidden" problems afterward that she can directly link to a failure on your part to tell her everything she needed to know. If her problem with the product or service is something that you should have told her about, you will find yourself faced not only with a returned item, but an angry female customer who won't buy from you again and who will tell others not to buy from you either.

Let me repeat again: women have *no problem* returning items! A man may stow it in the attic, keep it hidden away in a garage or trunk, or use it even if it doesn't work well rather than waste more time returning it or admitting he made a wrong decision. Not a woman—she will bring it back pronto!

> There is absolutely no use hiding information from a woman. You will just end up filling out the return forms and paperwork at a later date.

What a waste of time—both hers and yours—plus you lost both a commission and a client.

Sometimes salespeople ask me, "Do you mean we should actively point out what's wrong with a product?" If you're selling the right product to the right person, you shouldn't have to. What you have to do is help her make the right decision given her needs, set realistic expectations for the product, and outline the pros and cons in terms of how the product will solve her problem. This is how you show your trustworthiness and gain credibility.

When I bought my new phone, the salesman provided a perfect example of this. He listened carefully as I explained what I needed, asking a few pertinent questions about what I was looking for and what I wanted—the typical needs assessment. But then he did something a bit different. He asked me what I absolutely hated about my last phone. I had a list of things, of course, and I loved the opportunity to vent to such an attentive listener. (He was definitely making me feel like PART OF THE PROCESS.) After listening to what I liked and didn't like, he shared both the pros and cons of each phone as it related to what I had told him concerning my specific needs, likes, and dislikes. I didn't have to drag the negatives out of him. When I finally narrowed it down to the phone I wanted, he immediately went back to the one negative the phone had and showed me what I could do to correct the problem and make it work for me. I left feeling he had helped me make an informed, good decision—with no little surprises waiting for me when I started using the phone.

Any woman who is considering buying from you has enough to manage without having to manage you too, making sure you're going to deliver what you promise. She won't want the sales process to take twice as long as it should because she has to hunt for information or check up on everything you say. Remember, she wants it to be PRODUCTIVE. She won't want to get to the end of the sale and suddenly find a stack of hidden fees to be argued over. And she won't want to walk away wondering what else you didn't tell her, what fine print she overlooked. Remember: transparent, obvious, direct, and straightforward.

Tip #3: Don't Act Desperate

This is a tough one, because sometimes in sales, let's face it, we are desperate. It's the last day of the quarter and you need three more sales to hit your quota or to get the big bonus. So you put on your best outfit, fix an extra-big smile in place, practice your smoothest sales lines, and hit the floor. The problem is that the customers can see this coming a mile away—so they run in the other direction as quickly as humanly possible. The reality is that people want to work with, be with, and buy from SUCCESSFUL people—and anything that reeks of desperation will kill the deal. Men smell desperation and go in for the kill, expecting the greatest deal of all time—because, well, you'll do almost anything to get the sale. Women just find it worrisome, tedious, pitiful, suspicious, and a bit suffocating. Not one good word in that bunch, is there?

Psychologically, our sales style comes from one of two places: desperation or confidence. And confidence is what sells. Not ego or arrogance, just pure confidence in yourself and your product. When you feel and, as a result, *act* desperate, you begin trying too hard to make us trust you, like you, want to buy from you. Women interpret this as untrustworthiness because (1) it seems like you're uncomfortable, nervous, high-strung, or pushy, just as you'd be if you had something to hide; and (2) it seems as if you'll do whatever is necessary to make the sale happen—even if it means lying or exaggerating.

A story comes to mind from a few years ago when there was a serious hailstorm and our roof was damaged and needed to be replaced. Several contractors and roofers left their information or brochures in our mailbox and we began to sort through it all. We needed to make a decision quickly, but we wanted to make the right decision so we wouldn't have to go through the process again. When we finally narrowed it down to two companies, we set up an appointment with each. The first contractor was cordial, prepared, and knowledgeable, but explained up front that due to all the insurance claims, his calendar was filling up quickly. He suggested that we give him a call as soon as possible to set up a date and then he left, handing us a list of neighborhood references and putting the ball into our court. My impression was that he was good at his job and felt strongly about doing a good job, but he had tons of business so if we wanted him it was up to us to make the next move. He seemed extremely confident and in control.

The second contractor was just the opposite. He was hurried and not as prepared. But the worst was he started to push us to sign a contract before he even told us about his service or company. He kept telling us how much work he had and how busy he was, but he acted just the opposite. I felt like he desperately needed this job. And my thought was, "If he's this desperate *now* with hundreds of roofs to fix, how good could he really be?" It didn't feel right, and sure enough, when I checked his references, which I had to beg him for, I got nothing but bad reviews.

A female customer is looking for solutions to her shopping needs, not a bunch of new problems.

Think of your sales encounter as a job interview: Would you hire someone who told you he wanted the job because he was broke and no one else would hire him? Probably not, because if his situation is that bad, there's probably a good reason for it.

Now you might think that there's a fine line between trying hard and trying too hard. Not really. Trying hard is great customer service—trying too hard is desperation. Women want you to try hard to give them the best information. They want you to try hard to make the transaction enjoyable and the process easy. Women want you to try hard to be a good person who makes them feel good about working with you. If you are a good person with a good product and a good sense of how to help women learn about the product, then they will most likely trust what you say until you prove otherwise. But when you begin to try too hard, you begin to make people nervous and suspicious and they will want out.

How do you know when you are trying too hard? With women buyers it's pretty easy to tell. She doesn't answer you. She stops making eye contact. She doesn't return your calls or respond to your e-mails. She becomes defensive. She seems annoyed. Read the clues and watch her body language. When you start feeling like she's lost interest in you, guess what? She has. And no amount of chasing after her is going to make it better. Now you have two choices: you can put the blame on her, or you can step back and try to figure out if she left because she wasn't ready to buy or if she left because you literally drove her away with your desperate need to close the deal. Have the confidence to analyze your behavior in situations like this and then make the necessary changes to close more sales in the future.

Tip #4: Be Careful with the Upsell

Upselling is an important and lucrative part of sales strategy if used and done appropriately and honestly. There are many legitimate features and add-ons to products and services that can genuinely help customers achieve better results and more satisfaction from their purchase. And women will appreciate knowing these options. But there are also many tempting opportunities to pad the sale with unnecessary and even worthless features. Again we are talking about trust—and her need to be able to trust that when you suggest that she purchase bigger, better, fancier, or more expensive alternatives, you have her best interests in mind and not just your commission and quota. You may be extremely persuasive—you probably are if you're successful in this business, and it's easy to just stay on a roll and keep adding to a purchase. And if you are really good and she trusts you, you may find that she believes in you enough to buy additional items, warranties, or services, only to find out later that she really didn't need them at all. If that's the case, then you risked your reputation and the opportunity for a repeat customer and great, positive advertising for the price of an add-on. Not a good investment in your future.

Unfortunately, women are often easier targets for upselling than men for a few reasons. For one, if a women is enjoying the experience, she is not nearly as anxious to get out and on her way. She is more willing to stay longer and listen harder. Two, she really wants to make the right decision; therefore, if you make her believe that she really *needs* to have the things you are suggesting, she might be tempted to buy. Three, although women may enjoy shopping more, they also consolidate tasks more, and she usually finds it easier to buy everything at once rather than to have to come back and get the rest later. Men are more apt to buy "just what I came for" and leave.

So most salespeople have quickly figured out that upselling to a woman can be a profitable endeavor—or is it? Not if she doesn't really need or want what you are selling. You're just fooling yourself. When she realizes she bought more than she needed (or her friends or family point out she bought more than she needed) she will either come back to you with a return or never come back to you at all. Look at the Home Shopping Network, which is geared mainly toward women—it's a whirlwind of upselling. Every item is priced, then repriced with a bonus item, then repriced again with three travel sizes, and a bonus on top of the bonus until you can't even tell what the original item was. But as more salespeople try this trick, women are getting smarter about it.

The primary reason upselling poses a danger to your relationship is the feelings it produces in your female customer later. Don't ever underestimate the guilt factor in women. If a woman buys more than she needs or pays more than she should, she will quickly realize it and feel *bad* about the entire purchase. She will feel like you took advantage of her trust to lead her into excess, and it will make her angry—at herself for buying it and at you for convincing her to do it. You will stop being the friend and reliable salesperson who helped her and become someone to warn all her friends and family to stay away from. After all, you know more about your products than she does, and you didn't look out for her best interests, which is what a trustworthy person does.

A good example of the breach of trust through unnecessary upselling often comes up with warranties. Everyone is offering warranties on everything. There are probably warranties guaranteeing your warranties. But most experts will tell you that they are not worth the money, even as many salespeople try to persuade or scare you into buying them. Recently I was buying a new television at a well-known chain electronics store. A young man was explaining the pros and cons of flatscreen TVs to me. I really liked him. He was friendly and energetic and had a great sense of humor. He listened to what I wanted and narrowed it down quickly to three TVs. Then he gave me a very honest assessment of what I would probably like and not like about each after hearing exactly what I wanted. He didn't try to upsell, even when I asked about a more expensive model. Instead, he told me that for what I wanted, I didn't need the extras the other TV offered. (Sometimes "downselling" is the best way to make a sale!)

As I was paying, I braced myself for the warranty pitch I was prepared *not* to fall for. But he surprised me by saying, "Look, there is a warranty on this that I need to offer to you, but this has been a very reliable TV and you shouldn't have any problems in the next two years." Selling warranties is very profitable, so he might have been fired on the spot if someone from his company had overheard him. However, I have since bought another TV, a digital camera, and a video camera—and because I knew I could trust this young salesman, I've bought them all from him. I have spent far more money on other purchases than on the cost of one TV warranty. His company should give him a raise! When offering other products or services, focus on those features or elements that will be beneficial to her, not just what will earn you the most cash.

Of all the qualities you can bring to your job as a salesperson, the one that will pay off most is trustworthiness.

 Upselling when it's not in her best interests makes you a little more money today at the risk of losing a *lot* more money down the line.

Giving her honest, unbiased advice is more than just the right thing to do—it's an investment in your future prospects.

Deal Breaker #5

SHE DOESN'T THINK YOU'RE THE RIGHT PERSON FOR THE JOB

QUIZ

Be honest!

1. Have you ever referred a customer to a colleague who you believed was more qualified to help her? Did you do it of your own accord, or did the customer point out that you weren't meeting her needs?

2. Do you think your male customers are more knowledgeable about the products you sell than your female customers? How does that affect how you work with them?

3. How many magazines or journals do you read that cover the latest trends in your industry? Do you read all of the new marketing materials about the products you sell as soon as they are available?

4. How often do your female customers contact you about issues that occur after the sale, such as delayed delivery, faulty product, or disappointment with the end result? How often do your male customers involve you? Do you make yourself available to help customers with these issues?

5. How many of your female customers are repeat customers? What do you do to let them know that you would like their repeat business?

In general it is a woman's job to make sure that she surrounds herself with people who can be counted on to do what is necessary to help her and those she loves. I have my special "team" of vendors: Frank at the dry cleaners, Sophie at the salon, Greg at the pharmacy, Karen at the travel agency, and Joy at my favorite clothing store. I am loyal to these people because they have proven to me over and over that they are the right people for the job. Take note that I did *not* say I was necessarily loyal to the entire shop, store, or agency. There are many hairdressers at my salon, but I will delay my appointment to make sure I get Sophie. There are other travel agents, but I will patiently wait on hold until Karen is available. I've let other people go ahead of me at the drugstore in order to speak with Greg. And I don't ever shop for clothing on Tuesday because that is Joy's day off. Why? Because I am willing to wait, delay, and be inconvenienced to make sure I have exactly the right person for the job. How did I come to the conclusion that they were the only ones who could satisfy my needs? Because they did it successfully multiple times, and they've almost never let me down.

There is not a doubt in my mind that these people are absolutely right for the job I want done. I have a PERSONAL connection with each of them that goes beyond simply providing a service I need. They know what I like and don't like, what I need and don't need, and they give me personalized service every time, without fail. I also like and trust each one. They are all very PROFESSIONAL. Even though I feel like they are my friends, they are always right-on-target when it comes to doing business in an efficient, respectful way. In each case, I am PART OF THE PROCESS and they never hesitate to continue to ask questions and keep up with changes in my lifestyle. They make every call or visit PRODUCTIVE. They know what they are doing and are wonderfully knowledgeable about their specific product or service. They get right down to business even while we are sharing a joke or sharing news about our families. And I love that my experiences with them are so POSITIVE. They take the hassle out of planning a trip or even picking up a prescription. When I come across someone who fits all of my major criteria, they become my new best friend because I have found exactly the right person for the job.

I coach a lot of salespeople, and one of my clients recently called to let me know he had just changed companies. He had left the car industry and had gone into business with his brother in the furniture industry. He had always had a great sales record but now was disappointed that his "luck," as he put it, had run out. He wasn't closing many deals. "I'm likable, trustworthy, and respectful. I listen to their needs and I take a personal interest in my customers. What's going on?" I asked him a few questions about his new company and the new products he was selling, and I quickly identified the problem. "Brian, you are an excellent salesman. You have the drive, passion, and expertise. But Brian, you don't know your product yet. You haven't done your homework. You can't even answer basic questions about fabric, colors, styles, and manufacturers. All your past accolades and sales awards will not make up for your lack of knowledge about this particular product. As a woman, I don't believe you have the experience to help me make an informed decision and therefore I would not trust that you know what you're doing when it comes to selling me an entire room of new furniture. To be honest, Brian, right now you are *not* the right person for the job." But with some research and study, he could certainly change that.

There are two reasons why a woman might perceive that you aren't the right person for the job. One, you really *aren't* the right person for the job and you just haven't owned up to the fact that you need to learn more, train more, change companies or products, or refer another person who is better qualified in this instance. Or two, you are absolutely the right person for the job, but there is something about you that is causing her to doubt you and therefore view you as unqualified, in which case you need to do some serious self-analysis and fast!

Let's begin with the first situation, when she has you pegged as the wrong person for the job. As much as you don't want to admit it, she has you totally figured out and she's undeniably right about the fact that you aren't the *best* person to give her what she wants or needs. This is when knowing yourself and being honest with yourself about your capabilities comes in to play. How sad for both the salesperson and the client when we aren't sure (or we choose to ignore) right from the start that we aren't the answer to her problem. It's a waste of everyone's time and it makes us look foolish or even dishonest. When you know you aren't the right person for the job, you have to admit it, both to yourself and to her. That sounds awful, but there's a lot of benefit to be had in that kind of move. I'll explain more as we go on.

In the second scenario, let's say you *are* the right person for the job and you need to convince her of that. As I have said over and over, women are *constantly* evaluating whether you're worthy of the sale or not. If you want to close, you'll need to put all of your skills to work and avoid the deal breakers we've already discussed. But you will also have to exhibit your PROFESSIONAL knowledge and abilities, your commitment to making the buy PRODUCTIVE for her, and a willingness to learn more about her PERSONAL needs. See, a man might wait to make a final decision about you until he at least hears what you've got to offer and what the deal will be. In fact, if a salesperson appears to be incompetent, many men will consider buying from him anyway on the possibility of getting a great deal. Remember, sales is often a game for men. Having an opponent so easy to beat might not be as much fun, but hey, a win is a win.

Women have much less tolerance for disorganized, unknowl-edgeable, or incompetent salespeople. Women are looking at the future and seeing a very unpleasant experience ahead of them; men are looking at a result that could very well end in their favor. I was out to dinner once with a friend of mine and her son who was home from college. The service at the restaurant was terrible. She and I were getting more and more annoyed by the minute, yet he seemed perfectly fine. Finally she turned to him and said, "Doesn't this bother you at all?" He answered, "No, at school this kind of restaurant is our dream. Bad service means a free dinner." We were looking at the total experience, and he was looking at the end result.

Since women do come at a purchase from a holistic view-point, you can't discount or sweet-talk your way into a sale if you're incompetent or she thinks you are. You have to zero in on what's making her dismiss you and find a way to fix it. Often this comes under the heading of PROFESSIONAL qualifications, but there's a good chance it might be PART OF THE PROCESS as well.

So how do you convince a woman that you are indeed the RIGHT person for the job? The tough part of this deal breaker is that there are many off-putting things you could be doing dozens of times a day, yet never hear about it from your female customers. When a woman decides you're not the right person for the job, she doesn't usually say so—she just wants to get out of there with as little awkwardness as possible. Granted, if you really mess up, she may complain to your boss, but for minor infractions, she'll proba-bly just make an excuse to leave, say she's not ready to buy, come up with an "appointment" she forgot, or simply leave the store when you're not looking. So you will have to be confident enough to take a close look at yourself because you will probably have to decide on your own that you may be the problem and work to fix it.

The tips I'll share for avoiding this deal breaker cover both the scenarios described here. The first two focus on what to do when you aren't the right person for the job. The rest focus on proving to her that you are.

Tip #1: Be Up Front and Honest About Your Ability to Meet Her Needs

I have already told you two stories about how important it is to be honest about your ability to do the kind of job the client expects and deserves. In the first, I was realistic about what I could and couldn't do for my client, and instead of speaking on a topic that was outside of my area of expertise, I chose instead to refer another speaker, and I closed the deal anyway, got a ton of referrals, and a long-term positive result. In the second, I didn't share my concerns about presenting a serious topic in an inappropriate time slot—a mistake I will never forget or make again. There is nothing worse in sales than to overpromise and underdeliver—they destroy both our self-respect and reputation in one quick blow. Salespeople often tell me that rejection is the worst thing they might have to deal with—and I say, "Not at all. Sales and rejection come hand in hand, but a destroyed reputation is much, much worse." We can always make sure that the reason someone did not buy from us had nothing to do with our ethics, our ability to deliver, and our commitment to good service. Remember: It's not just about closing the deal; it's about closing the *right* deal, which means making sure you are the right person for the job and that you're willing to admit it if you aren't.

Now, just because you don't want to promise you can do something you can't, that doesn't mean that you shouldn't challenge or stretch yourself into new areas. For instance, when I first started speaking professionally, I had forty-five minutes of good presentation material. I now have fifteen hours of solid, funny, insightful information on a variety of topics. The only way I improved was to constantly try out new stories, add new information, experiment with techniques, and constantly push myself to explore new subjects and topics. But I am very aware that there are some subjects (economics still being one of those) that I simply don't have the interest or expertise to attack. The key to expanding your abilities is to keep learning new things, and I'll talk more about that later.

How do you know the difference between challenging yourself and learning new things and simply getting in over your head and letting a client down? Two words: feedback and results.

If you've successfully pushed yourself to go to the next level and met your customer's needs, she will give you great feedback and the results will be a sale plus a long-term customer.

If you simply deceived yourself and her and promised what you couldn't deliver, the feedback won't be pleasant and the result will be that you don't make a sale. So it is very important that you know the difference. My best advice is to trust your gut and get your ego out of the way. I believe that deep down you know when you are capable of delivering what you are promising and when you aren't. It's not much fun to be in over your head. It's scary, worrisome, and extremely stressful to oversell, knowing the results will be a lost sale, an angry customer, and even perhaps the loss of a job. So be honest with what you know and don't know, what you can and cannot do, and what you can and cannot deliver—that is what she is expecting and what she deserves.

A few years ago I was redoing all of my marketing materials. I contracted with a woman who had been referred to me. When we met I was blown away by her creativity. Her style was professional and refreshing, just the unique look I was going for. I told her how rushed I was, that I needed the new materials quickly because I was sending out a proposal to a new client in three weeks, and that I wanted it to look perfect. She said that was no problem so we started to finalize the deal. She fit all my criteria. She had even heard me speak at a recent event and knew my style. She also seemed so honest with me, never afraid to tell me if an idea I had was the wrong way to go or something else would work better.

So I handed over all the information she needed *plus* my complete faith that a quality job would get done on time. I was so convinced that she was on board that I left on a two-week vacation with her promise that she would have all the designs and proofs for me to look at by the time I got home. Then we could send them immediately to the printer so everything would be ready in time. I was confident that I had hired the right person, and I never worried once during my vacation. Boy was I wrong! When I got home, I couldn't reach her. I left her several messages, which she never returned. I finally stopped by her house and she said she was hurrying to a meeting but would call me that night, which she never did. *Finally*, the truth began to sink in. She hadn't done the work at all and was avoiding me. When I told a friend of mine who knew her what had happened she said, "I'm not surprised. She and her husband recently separated and she's having some problems with one of her kids who is in trouble at school. She has a lot going on right now."

I finally confronted her almost a week later (three weeks after our verbal agreement and on the exact day the project was to have been completed!), and she confessed that she hadn't had the time or the emotional energy to get to my project yet. She apologized profusely, gave me way too many details on all the problems she was having at home, and then said that she would be ready to start the work the next day. I answered, "Thanks, but no thanks. I've already given the project to someone else."

Now before you peg me as a person who is not very compassionate or empathetic of other people's problems, that is so not the case. My anger and disappointment stemmed from the fact that she had not been honest with me from the beginning. I *loved* her work—had she truthfully explained the situation and told me her time line, I very well may have decided to work with her anyway. Or I may have decided I couldn't wait this time, but I would definitely use her for my new website, which was my next project. If she had told me the truth—that she was not the right person at that moment in her life to successfully meet my needs and time-frame—she could have still kept me as a client, either for this project or the next one. But, she chose to *not* share all the information I needed to make an informed decision, and it cost me three valuable weeks and the opportunity to meet the goal I had set. It was an unPROFESSIONAL thing to do and a breach of my PERSONAL trust. That, for a woman, is not usually forgivable.

How is this different for a man? When I told a male friend what had happened he felt no sympathy for me. Instead he said, "Well, that was pretty stupid of you. I always give a deadline much sooner than I really need it because I figure most people are usually late!" Men often calculate in the possibility of people failing to do what they say they will do. That way they are seldom surprised when people's lack of professionalism shows through—and they have prepared for it. But I took her at her word. And you need to know that, for a woman, that's pretty big stuff. It may take you a while to get her trust back again, if ever.

You may have to jump through a few hoops to persuade her that you are a likable, knowledgeable, and respectful person. But, in the end, if you make it through—you better *follow through* and be the person she expects you to be.

There is one more thing to consider when determining if you're the right fit for a client, and that's determining if she's the right fit for you. Often salespeople are so busy trying to be the right person that they fail to turn the situation around. I have definitely learned to say no to any client when I have doubts about a successful partnership. If you think there's a good chance that the customer is going to walk away from the experience unsatisfied, not because of anything specifically that you might or might not do, but just because her expectations and your expectations for the process are completely different, it's better to be honest about that up front than to earn a reputation for not meeting a customer's expectations. Sometimes there are customers I just know won't be pleased no matter what I do. Perhaps we have different goals, or our business styles or personalities just don't mesh. These are the customers that I try to refer to someone else. A good tip here is that if you don't like a customer, then the chances are good they won't like you either. If you don't trust them, then the feeling is probably mutual. Although we salespeople try our best to find a way to get along with everyone, sometimes we just have to admit that there are people we just won't work well with. In those cases, we need to match them up with someone else who can work with them rather than push through and face the predictable negative consequences.

Know what you can and can't do. Know your strengths and weaknesses and own up to them. Know what your product can and can't do for her. Know your schedule, your time line, the availability of your resources, your budget, and your ability to satisfy her 100 percent. Make sure you and what you are selling are exactly what she needs. And if you aren't meeting her needs, be the one to help her, lead her, or introduce her to the *right* person who can.

Tip #2: If You Can't Do It, Get Her to the Person Who Can

I realize that I have mentioned this before, but it is worth discussing in more depth because this is a really tough concept for most salespeople. They are so busy trying to go after every prospect that the thought—the mere mention—that maybe we should pass one of our own potential customers to another salesperson (our competition, in a way) is almost more than we can fathom. But honestly, sometimes the only *right* thing to do for you and the customer is to refer her to someone who would be a better fit.

In life there is a constant pull between our ego's voice (I want to do it my way, I am right, this is good for me, I deserve this more, I want to win) and the drive to do what's best for everybody (there's plenty for everyone, it's okay to ask for help, I could do this better, I could be wrong), especially in the arena of sales. As we discussed before, ego is a necessary part of successful sales—when it is balanced by the ability to admit we're wrong, be open to new ideas, and be assured that working together can benefit everyone. If you refuse to ever let a customer go or find it impossible to team her up with someone else better qualified when the situation calls for it, it will catch up with you. You will find yourself dealing with a customer who feels disappointed and misled.

As much as I hate to admit it, this is where women often make a mistake in the buying process. If and when she decides that you passed all of her initial tests, she may just *assume* you are the right person without questioning it any further. In other words, once she decides to trust you, she really *does* trust that you will be able to get the job done. If she finds out you aren't the right person, she will feel extremely disappointed and let down. You've wasted her time as well as betrayed her trust.

 In sales, reputation is your most important asset. Concentrate on doing the right thing by her—even if it means that once in a while you have to admit that someone else might be able to help her better than you can.

Not too long ago I spoke to two insurance companies in the same week. Both audiences were salespeople who sold many different products in many different market segments. Both events were incentive trips for their top performers as a reward for a great year and high sales numbers. But that was where the similarities stopped. I always attend the reception the evening before I speak to get a good feel for the group and have a chance to meet and visit with some of the people. The first reception seemed different from the moment I walked in. It was dark and quiet, not very energetic or fun. And everyone pretty well stayed together in small groups and basically hung out just with the people from their office or region. As I moved around meeting people, I overheard a lot of complaining—about the company, the products, and the sales expectations for the upcoming year. What they really were griping about the most were the people who received awards at the banquet the night before. Many of them seemed really angry and upset at some of the people who had been recognized. I also heard lots of excuses: "Well, if I had her territory" or "He has a bigger budget" (or lower prices, better customer base—just fill in the blanks and add whatever excuse you can think of).

Now I have to say I wasn't surprised because I had learned during my conference call that this company's philosophy toward sales was rooted in pitting each salesperson against the other with no incentives in place to work as a team or help each other out. Every salesperson was expected to know every product and there was little or no encouragement to work together or share information with other salespeople. As a result, it was not surprising to find them acting territorial, standoffish, jealous, and resentful even in a social situation—it just mirrored their professional behavior.

The second group, three nights later, was totally the opposite. Their culture emphasized the team. Their goal was to service the customer the best way possible, and they had discovered it worked best when their sales force pooled their resources, product knowledge, and expertise. So if I happened to be a customer and I was working with one of them whose background was life insurance and I began inquiring about disability insurance, it would be perfectly acceptable (and applauded) if he/she picked up the phone and dialed a colleague and either asked for help, set up a meeting with the three of us, or possibly even turned me over to that person for that particular portion of my insurance needs. Great for the customer—it meant they always had the *right* person for the job.

As a result, even the atmosphere at the evening reception was amazingly different. This group was animated and happy. They moved freely around the room, kidding and having fun with their colleagues. They were congratulating each other on their awards and seemed genuinely fond of one another. As I spoke to many of them throughout the evening I realized that they really liked having the opportunity open to them to refer their customers to other people. They enjoyed the mutual benefit of having customers referred back to them. In fact, many of them had left other companies and came to work for this one because they realized that they couldn't always be everything to everyone. One salesman said, "At first it was hard. I was used to the old school—keep all the sales to myself. Don't ever even let another salesperson know your customer's name. Do what you do the best and wing the rest and hope it works out. Here I feel good. If I don't know something, I can pick up the phone and have an answer or another person's help immediately."

Don't be afraid to ask for help or to refer your customer to someone who can get the job done better. Believe me, I know this isn't easy. I want to close every sale. I don't want to lose a customer. But I've learned from experience that it's the better choice in the long run to do what is the absolute *best* for the customer. Doing the right thing always works out in the end.

Bottom line: If you aren't the right person, then find the right person. It's just the right thing to do.

Tip #3: Know Your Stuff

So now we're going to assume that you are the right person for the job, and either she doesn't know it yet or you think she doubts it. How are you going to prove it to your female customer? If she has done her homework and done the research *before* she meets you, then you had better not only know your stuff but also know it better than she does. If she is clueless and doesn't know where to even begin, then you had better be able to explain it in a way that makes sense. Either way, the spotlight is on you to prove to her that you know what you are doing.

Remember, she is interviewing you as well as your product, and your inability to answer whatever concerns or questions she has with strong, honest, and knowledgeable answers will annoy her and turn her off. This is definitely *not* the time to be vague, confused, overwhelmed, or just plain unsure.

You would think a complete understanding of what one is selling would be a given, a prerequisite to the job. Unfortunately, that's not always the case.

 Selling is a lot like being in school for the rest of your life.

If your company and product or service is going to stay competitive, there are going to be constant changes. New product lines will be added, improvements will be made, and some things will be discarded totally to make room for the new items. And just like the teacher who is ready to ask you a question in front of the class when you aren't prepared, women are ready to do the same.

Don't men ask questions, too? Not nearly as many and for different reasons. I think in many cases men just don't have the desire to know every little detail as much as women do. But men also are more concerned about being in charge of the buying situation. They are not nearly as ready to hand it over to the salesperson as women are. Again remember, women don't view this as a competition where one person has to win—so asking questions to them is simply a means of making sure that their decision to buy is on-target and they have indeed found the right item.

How do you make sure you can answer most questions? Read everything you can about your industry. Subscribe to industry newsletters and magazines. I read everything I can whenever I can about psychology, human behavior, relationships, sales, and leadership. No matter how much education or experience we have, the world is moving too fast for us to keep up unless we decide that learning is a continuous process that will never end. We owe it to our clients to be as in-the-know and up-to-date as possible.

> We are no longer just in sales. We are educators, consultants, advisers, and futurists. We need to sell our products and services within a total context of offering solutions to problems.

We need to look at the big picture and not just the single sale. And that means we can never stop learning. It always amazes me how many salespeople don't subscribe to any trade journals and magazines about their industry or how many whine about taking classes or in-services offered to them for *free* by their companies. We can't afford to be behind the competition and out of the loop when it comes to new ideas and solutions for the future.

 Our clients are counting on us to be the absolute experts in our field and they have a right to expect that they can turn to us for help, advice, and answers.

Move outward from what you know and get help or advice from people who know more than you do. I love to surround myself with people who are smarter, more talented, more creative, and more technology savvy than I am. At every level of my career I have sought out mentors and experts who are willing and excited to take me to the next level. It amazes and saddens me to speak at conventions and hear salespeople gripe and complain about the new products or the upcoming training or their new computer system. I often ask them, "Don't you realize that if your company wasn't going through constant reevaluation and change, it wouldn't be able to stay in business and you would be out of a job?" In order to be considered the right person for the job, you had better be at the top of your field, with the latest and best information about your product/service and the confidence and expertise to convince me that I can count on you to deliver exactly what you promise.

Aside from knowledge of your own product, you should also be prepared to give information and answer questions about how your product compares to the competition. You have to be accurate, and you have to do it while resisting the temptation to say negative things about them. A woman will react much better when you tell her what is great about your product and why it is the best choice for her than if you concentrate on telling her the negative things about someone else's product. You can tell her about the differences—"they do that" and "we do this," but let your product sell itself on its merits, not on the deficiencies of something else. If you can explain the strengths and advantages of your product compared to others, she'll begin to trust your answers much more and believe that you're genuinely trying to help her make the right decision.

What if you haven't had enough time on the job or in the territory to build an extensive knowledge base? What if you don't know the answers to every question she'll ask? Just when I think I have every aspect of a topic covered, a client will come up with a different slant or idea that they want integrated, and I am in the process of relearning again. Which is okay—once in a while! While women are very impressed when you have all the data at your fingertips, they do understand that sometimes you don't. Remember, her questions aren't meant to trip you up. She certainly wants to know that you are on top of your product for the most part, but women are pretty good at recognizing that we don't always have all the answers. She will just expect that you take seriously any questions you can't answer, keep track of them, and get back to her with an answer as soon as possible. She will not appreciate having to track you down or remind you to get information. If you are the right person for the job, then you will make it a number one priority to take care of business and see that her questions are handled, whether by you or someone else.

Keep a strong network of colleagues, industry experts, websites, and other resources handy. In fact, exhibiting a desire to educate yourself or include others in the process can demonstrate your commitment to providing better information or service in the future. On the other hand, if you let your lack of knowledge fluster you or cause you to make excuses, she may tire of you very quickly.

Some salespeople have trouble answering a woman's questions, not because they don't know the answer, but because they're used to dealing with men's techniques of asking a question as a test and challenge to the salesperson. When they respond to women's informational questions, they take on a defensive, aggressive, confrontational tone. Not good. I think this comes from the old sales strategy still being taught that a good salesperson must overcome the objections in order to close the deal. Therefore many salespeople perceive any question as an objection or criticism of the product so they become aggressive in their attempt to convince the woman that she is wrong and they are right.

It is very important for you to know that women are rarely testing you, criticizing you, objecting to you, or setting you up to fail with their questions. They ask questions because they really want to know more about you, the product, your company, or the financing. Remember, this isn't a contest of wills with her—a game of who wins and who doesn't—she is trying to understand and fit all the information into the big picture.

She wants more than just answers—she wants to feel that her questions were taken seriously and responded to with respect and thoughtfulness, so any annoyed, aggressive, or defensive attitude is almost guaranteed to put her off.

I have often coached male salespeople who struggle with this issue a lot and are the first to admit it. They begin by telling me that they don't like selling to women because women treat them as if they don't know what they are doing and it is insulting to them. When I ask for an example, they invariably start telling me about all the questions. As one male computer salesperson said to me, "It's as though women don't trust me at all—like they think I don't understand anything about computers." "No," I told him, "if a woman is asking that many questions it is because *she* doesn't understand computers and wants to know more." He was taking her questions as an insult, when it was just the opposite. She needed and expected him to be the one with the answers so he could help her.

For women, asking questions and getting answers are just PART OF THE PROCESS in order for her to make sure that both you and the product are the right choice. If you can handle her questions PROFESSIONALLY and treat them as simply an attempt to learn more and not an objection you have to overcome, you will get a lot closer to gaining a customer and closing the deal.

Tip #4: Make It Happen

Sometimes you have to go beyond the norm and do more than expected to be considered the right person for the job—especially when your competition is a good company with an excellent reputation and competitive prices. It's going to take some creativity and great customer service to stand out and be the one she chooses. Women *love* great customer service and will respond with appreciation, and most likely a sale, when she finds someone who goes the extra mile.

A friend of mine recently bought new gutters for her house. In the process, she spoke with two competing salesmen who knew each other and each other's products very well, because they had worked in the same territory for a number of years. The first—we'll call him Michael—had the more expensive product. The second, Alex, had a slightly lower-quality product, but with a better price point. Both men, however, represented established, well-respected brands. Because these were gutters (not the most interesting or fun things to buy), she had pretty much decided to go with the lower-priced company because, well, there really wasn't much else that set them apart but the price. However, two days later I noticed the crew of the more expensive company at her house putting up new gutters.

When I asked her what made her change her mind, she told me what had happened. She had explained to both salesmen that although she wanted to start work right away, she had one problem. There was a tree with an overhanging branch in her yard and that needed to be taken care of before work could begin. The next day, Michael called and said, "I'd love your business. I can arrange, with your permission, for a friend of mine to take care of your tree situation and I can just include that as part of the estimate I gave you. That way you don't have to worry about it and we can get your new gutters up before the weekend." Wow! He could take care of her problem without her even lifting a finger or asking for help. As a result, his price immediately became more competitive. When she figured in the cost, time, and effort to find a tree trimmer, wait for him to show up, then pay him—not to mention the hassle involved—well, there was no contest. Going the extra mile closed the deal.

For my friend, the PERSONAL connection was there—she really liked the fact that Michael had listened to her problem, heard her concern about dealing with the tree, and took charge. He definitely made her feel like he was the right person for the job. If he could handle this problem, then he could handle anything else that might come up. But, in their second meeting, it was the PROFESSIONAL and PRODUCTIVE aspects of the relationship that really sealed the deal. Michael was knowledgeable, honest, and straightforward. He knew his product, his competitor's product, her options for financing, the homeowner's association rules and regulations that governed gutters and roofing, and he instilled a sense of trust that the job would be done right and on time. His willingness to be involved in the project as a whole overcame her resistance to the price because it saved her time, money, and hassle, and it had taken another item off of her endless to-do list. She was relieved, impressed, and satisfied—and she told everyone at the next homeowner's meeting about it! (Remember, word-of-mouth marketing among women is more than a habit, it's a phenomenon.)

How is a man different? When I told several guys I knew about what had happened, they almost unanimously said, "Well, if it were me, I would have just cut down the tree myself and gone with the cheaper guy." Well, what is there for me to say to that? Other than I wouldn't want to bet on how long it would take for them to really get a ladder and a chain saw, climb up on the roof, cut down a huge branch without killing themselves, then cut it into smaller pieces of wood, put it in the back of a borrowed pickup truck, and figure out where to take it. The old gutters would probably still be right where they were a year from now.

You don't have to be a superhero to make every sale. But going the extra mile really makes a difference to a woman, and it produces feelings of gratitude, surprise, and relief that she'll remember for a long time. Remember, women want the process to be easy and smooth, and they're relying on you to make it happen.

 If there's an obstacle you can knock out of the way quickly to save her valuable time, she'll take notice and probably reward you with a sale.

In a practical sense, you can utilize this strategy by always looking for new, better ways to solve problems, especially unique problems. If, like Michael, you can find a way to make your customer's life easier, that proves you're thinking about her as an individual, not just a bottom-line signature. It reinforces the PERSONAL connection even as it opens up new ways to make the sale PRODUCTIVE. Look at each case from the customer's angle, but apply your objective viewpoint and expert knowledge. What will she need that she doesn't know about? How can you make things easier for her in the future, when she runs into the issues she won't see now? How could you remove the issues that are there—do you offer special financing or partnerships with installers and repairmen? You have the inside knowledge and the professional resources to get things done that she can only dream of—use them, and she'll know for sure no one else could make her time more PRODUCTIVE than you.

Another way to increase your productivity is to get rid of dead weight. Don't overcomplicate the process; so many salespeople do this. Make it about her—not about the system. Eliminate unnecessary paperwork. Give her straightforward pros and cons to help her make efficient decisions. Steer her toward helpful associates and make time to follow up. Often it's only at the end of a sale or after a sale that women can break down and analyze the entire process logically, and she may have some insight that will help you win the next female customer who walks through the door. (Women like to help the right person do his or her job—let them, and you'll find you get a lot of PRODUCTIVE advice!) Remember, women like most shopping to be fun, and if they are shopping for something that isn't fun at all (like gutters or air conditioners or life insurance policies), then they want it to be easy.

Keep it simple—not intellectually simple—but keep the process simple. She has a lot of people to choose from. Will she choose you? Will you prove to be the best person for the job—the one who is dependable, trustworthy, empathetic, and willing to get her what she needs with the least amount of hassle possible? If so, she will not only become your customer but the best public relations spokesperson you could have. Believe me, it's worth the time and effort to do whatever is necessary to bring in more female customers and to keep the ones you have.

Tip #5: Show Her You're in It for the Long Haul

Have you ever heard a woman complain that someone just won't commit? There can be no doubt that most women are very into commitment—not just when it comes to personal relationships but also when it comes to her buying style and expectations. Think about everything I've been telling you that women want out of the sales experience. Well, it's hard work for women to find salespeople and companies that offer this type of experience; it takes a lot of time and energy. Women would just as soon not have to do all of that work every time they need a new product. They want to make things easier on themselves in the future. That means that when a female customer is evaluating you and your performance, she's evaluating your potential to fulfill her needs in the long term. She's looking for commitment, and you need to show her that you *are* committed—at least if you're interested in return business.

 A woman wants to feel that this sale will begin a long-term relationship with you and your business.

She's investing herself in this relationship by researching your company, evaluating you, giving you a shot at the sale. And now you need to show her that you're invested in her well-being, too. What's the point of her investing time and effort in your business if you're not investing an equal amount in her future success or happiness? Even if you do everything else right, she may still take her dollars elsewhere if she feels you're only in it for one sale and aren't going to be there for her the next time she needs you.

Sometimes, thinking about the long term means sacrificing in the short term—whether by selling her a lower-priced item that will do everything she needs, eating the cost to fix a mistake (remember my offer for free chrome wheels?), or even letting go of a sure deal to preserve a valuable relationship. But nine times out of ten it's worth it and will pay off with a female customer. Some salespeople complain that their companies don't have that mindset, so their hands are tied. It's get in, make the sale, get out, and move on to the next customer.

Well, even when that's the case, you still need to show her you're in it for the long haul if you want to make the sale and further your personal success. If you work for a more institutional style of business like a big-box store or a large sales organization, you might need a little imagination in addition to the suggestions below, but it can be done. Building a long-term relationship with your female customers means you're securing their future business, their goodwill, and their services as free publicists and marketers. Sound good? Ready to commit to your female customers? Here are some suggestions to jolt you out of the short-term mindset.

Be reliable and follow up. Remember, a woman feels that she has a lot of obligations, and if you can make her feel slightly less responsible by taking on any extra work associated with her purchase, she'll know that you're committed to her satisfaction and overall well-being. So make sure she knows that she can count on you to be accountable for delivery, installation, or any other services. Even if you aren't the person doing it, make sure that it's getting done, and done well.

Following up with customers is critical, too. This is the most obvious show of long-term commitment, and there are lots of different ways to do it. For instance, you could ask customer services to notify you if any of your customers have complaints or returns, and follow up to make sure all is going well. Or you could make a point of greeting and chatting with customers you recognize, even if they're not looking to buy from your department. If you're in a more relationship-focused business, make sure you set aside time to call your customers after a visit or a sale, ask if they have any questions, and thus remind them that they enjoy working with you. And obviously, if you say you'll do something by a certain date, do it! That's just PROFESSIONAL.

Following up tells a woman that she's more than just a price tag to you, and that she made an impression on you—which will make an impression on her. It also puts you and your products back in her mind, so when she's thinking about what she needs next, your face is much more likely to pop up.

Be her advocate. This is a great way to prove your commitment! Take it a step further than just the follow up. Be proactive. The next time a woman buys from you, say, "If there are any problems with it, don't call customer service, call me. I'll help you get it resolved." This is an incredibly powerful statement, and let me tell you, it will definitely help you win repeat business. If a female customer feels that you're willing to go out of your way to make sure that she's happy with the products she buys from you, why wouldn't she buy from you now and in the future? You've shown her that you are PERSONALLY invested in her satisfaction. There's only one problem with this approach: You have to mean it. If you make this offer, but then don't return her phone calls, you've just earned yourself some bad word of mouth—PERSONALLY. This can't be an offer you make casually, so you will need to be selective. Read the customer, determine if she is somebody who really is looking for a long-term relationship, who buys a lot of what you sell, and who is likely to come and see you again.

Ask for referrals. Asking for referrals is a key part of most businesses, especially when you're facing women and their incredible ability to make or break a business based on word of mouth. But it also is one of the aspects of selling that many salespeople find uncomfortable. With women, it's a bit easier than with men; if she has had a great experience with you, she has every intention of talking about you and sharing your name and number with her friends and family anyway. So you don't have to make it so formal—just let her know how much you enjoyed working with her and tell her you would be delighted to help any of her friends and family. This enhances the idea in her mind that you would like to make this a long-term relationship. The fact of the matter is that involving a woman's inner circle by requesting to be referred to them will often solidify her positive opinion of you. Remember, women want to spread the word about you to the people they know and trust. So while asking for referrals is a great idea, *if* you've done an amazing job and she leaves impressed, she'll refer you anyway. She is the absolute best advertiser and promoter you could ever have.

Tip #6: LISTEN TO HER, LISTEN TO HER, LISTEN TO HER

Have I made it clear that you need to *listen* to her? This is the last tip in this book, not because it is the least important, but because it is so very important. Believe me when I say that even worse than a woman scorned is a woman who doesn't feel as though she has been heard *and* understood. I'm not saying that it's always easy to understand what a woman wants. In fact, sometimes we don't always know exactly what it is we want. That is why your role is so vital. Your single most important purpose is to find out what she wants, when she wants it, why she wants it, and then get it for her as quickly and easily as possible! Wow! No one said sales was easy. The good news is that being the right person for the job doesn't mean you are in this alone—this is a partnership. Knowing your stuff and being a know-it-all are two totally different things. You need to take the time to listen to her, without acting impatient or distracted—this is important—and find out what she is looking for. Sometimes this means reading between the lines. She may not always be perfectly clear because she is in the process of trying to figure it out herself. That is why women will often tell you the whole story about why they want it, who it's for, and why they need it today—they are trying to decide what is best for them and everyone else involved. And talking out loud and asking questions is a way for them to do that. It is a way of processing everything so she (with your help) can come up with the right answer. Your role is to prove to her that you know what you are talking about, you value her time, and you're dedicated to helping her make the right purchase.

Your mission should be to make sure she gets what she needs with as little hassle as possible.

That may mean that you will probably have to spend more time with her than you would a man. Often salesmen will tell me that they get frustrated with the "story" and the questions because it isn't getting them anywhere closer to closing the deal. How wrong they are! It is exactly the path, in fact sometimes the only path, to her making a decision to buy. The story is PART OF THE PROCESS for her. Remember how we said at the beginning that if she's still talking, you can probably still learn something to your benefit? This is your opportunity to find out what really will be the best thing for her needs and if she needs anything else from you she doesn't know about.

Even if it seems that the story she is telling you is just unnecessary background chatter, listen anyway. It may not seem connected to the business deal at hand, but she is really telling you a great deal about herself—information that could be useful in this sale when trying to match her with the right product or in a future sale. Move beyond understanding her needs to understanding who she is and why she might continue to buy from you in the long term. For her it's important that you know her background and a few things about her. If you don't, why would you care about helping her? It has to be about more than just your job, it has to be PERSONAL. And if you are interested in her personal story, she'll perceive that to mean you're interested in a long-term relationship. So when she starts talking, it is very important that you do not appear distracted, look at the time, watch someone outside the office, or fiddle with your paper. Listening means paying attention with your eyes, mind, and spirit.

Aside from that, I always tell men, "Look, both sexes take their own sweet time buying, just in different ways. Listening to her is crucial because it pulls everything else together."

 A woman may want to talk more and ask more questions, but she will not have the time or inclination to spend endless hours haggling over a few dollars on the price. A man may not talk much at all, but the end negotiation could take forever.

Listening is a sign of PERSONAL interest. Listening carefully and helping her identify what she needs and wants will make the process far more PRODUCTIVE. She will feel that you have made her PART OF THE PROCESS. And it is much easier to like someone and feel POSITIVE about working with them if they take the time to listen to your ideas and point of view. When you stop thinking about what you are going to say or do next to close the sale and turn your focus to her, you will become a collaborator, not a competitor. She will feel respected and will trust that you view her as the decision maker. Plus it will go a long way to setting you up as the *right* person for the job.

Turn Those Deal Breakers into Deal Makers

Well, there you have it. While I may not have answered the eternal question—what does a woman want?—I have certainly started you on the path to understanding what she wants when it comes to buying from you.

> Psychology can teach you so many things that the average sales training can't.

Delving into the psychology of human behavior—what makes people think the way they do, act the way they do, and react the way they do—is an absolutely vital process if you truly want to excel in sales. While men and women have many similarities when buying, now you also realize how many differences they bring to the process as well. And as much as this was a book about selling to women, you probably noticed early on that it was also very much a book about *you*.

What do you bring to the process? What fears, attitudes, and behaviors do you need to reassess or change in order for you to become more successful? How good are you at determining the personalities of your customers and working to sell in a way that they understand and can relate to? How flexible are you in terms of adapting to each unique situation? Do you trust your own instinct, or do you often let your ego lead the way? Do you want to simply win and close the deal, or do you want to create a lifelong customer and partner? Are you focused on the short term or do you make decisions based upon what's best in the long run?

These and many other questions are just part of the continuing learning process and journey for those of us who want to sell well, sell more, and sell for the right reason. So what are you waiting for? Eighty-five percent of your customers are women and they are ready to buy from you—are you ready to sell to them? If so, let the games stop and the collaboration begin. When you turn your deal breakers into deal makers, I promise that you have a great shot at making a fortune selling to women, and that's a win-win for everyone!

Connie Has a World of Resources Dedicated to Your Success . . .

One part success library and one part coaching tool, Connie Podesta's Success Resource Center offers you a comprehensive collection of her products (books, audio, CDs, DVDs, etc.) to help you reach higher levels of success in both your personal and professional life.

Below are two of Connie's other books you will certainly enjoy.

Life Would Be Easy if It Weren't for Other People

In this book, Connie shows how to develop healthy communication patterns with people who literally "drive you crazy." She analyzes why difficult people act the way they do, then describes how best to react to those people to move the relationship in a more positive direction. Connie includes practical strategies to help make all relationships work better for you—immediately! A must-read for anyone who is dealing with stressful or difficult people or who desires positive communication in their business and personal life.

How to Be the Person Successful Companies Fight To Keep

Based on a personal survey of hundreds of business owners, managers, and human resource professionals nationwide, this book by Connie focuses on the top eight high-performance behaviors employees must demonstrate to remain employable and marketable. Gain invaluable knowledge into the minds of employers and discover what you need to do to be an indispensable worker, one who is worth fighting to keep. Definitely recommended reading for anyone interested in the secrets of staying employed in today's precarious job market.

"An indispensable survival manual for employees today."
—*Business Times*

Discover all of the ways Connie can help you or your organization become more successful.
To order your success tools, please contact us at

conniepodesta.com
972-596-5501